Practice Book

GRADE 3-1

Harcourt

Orlando   Boston   Dallas   Chicago   San Diego

Visit *The Learning Site!*
www.harcourtschool.com

Contents

HIDDEN SURPRISES

Printed in the United States of America

ISBN 0-15-312712-0

7 8 9 10   054   2002   2001

Name _____

▶ **Complete each sentence with a word from the box.**

responsible	business	suggested
researched	creative	expect

Maria Writes a Story

1. Maria decided to write a new story of her own.

She wanted to be _____.

2. She decided to use her own ideas, instead

of the ideas her friends _____.

3. The main character, Matt, would own a _____.
He would fix other people's computers.

4. Matt needed people to trust him, so he tried hard to

be _____.

5. When Matt didn't know the answer to a question, he

_____ it. He looked it up on the Internet.

6. Sometimes Matt found answers that most people

would not _____.

▶ **Write two Vocabulary Words that could be used to describe a character.**

7. _____

8. _____

 TRY THIS! Think of a character for a story. Write a description of that character. Use at least three of the Vocabulary Words.

Harcourt

Name _____

▶ Fill in the first column of the chart as you read
"Arthur Writes a Story." After you have read the story,
fill in the second column. Tell what happens in time order.

Prediction Chart

What I Predict Will Happen	What Actually Happens

▶ Why is Arthur's first story his best story?

_____

_____

_____

Harcourt

Name _____

Breakable

Name _____

Prefix	Suffix	Meaning	Example
dis-		opposite of	dislike
non-		not	nonstop
over-		too much	oversleep
	-able	able to be	chewable
	-tion, -ion	the result of or state of	invention

► Add a prefix or a suffix from the box above to each underlined word below. Form a new word that means the same as the words in parentheses ( ). Write the new word on the line.

1. (charged too much) She was _____ for the cereal.

2. (able to break) Be careful with those _____ dishes.

3. (not poisonous) The snake I stepped on was _____.

4. (being celebrated) The birthday _____ was fun.

5. (not appear anymore) The snow seemed to _____ quickly.

6. (too crowded) The concert was noisy and _____.

► Add a prefix or a suffix to each word. Use the new word in a sentence.

7. drink _____

8. eat _____

Hidden Surprises 5

Name _____

▶ **Read the paragraphs and choose the prefix or the suffix that belongs with each underlined word. Fill in the oval next to your choice.**

Arthur likes writing fiction and **(1)** fiction. He always tries to tell an **(2)** enjoy story. He especially likes writing stories that are **(3)** believe. Sometimes he writes so much he gets **(4)** tired.

Arthur also likes a class **(5)** discuss. Once his teacher asked the class to talk and then to write about their future jobs. Arthur's **(6)** predict was that he would be a writer. His teacher gave his paper an *A*. Arthur was **(7)** joyed! He was in **(8)** belief when the teacher put his paper on the bulletin board.

1 ⬭ dis
⬭ non
⬭ over
⬭ able

2 ⬭ tion
⬭ able
⬭ dis
⬭ over

3 ⬭ ion
⬭ able
⬭ over
⬭ non

4 ⬭ ion
⬭ able
⬭ over
⬭ non

5 ⬭ ion
⬭ able
⬭ over
⬭ non

6 ⬭ dis
⬭ ion
⬭ over
⬭ able

7 ⬭ dis
⬭ non
⬭ over
⬭ able

8 ⬭ dis
⬭ over
⬭ able
⬭ non

Harcourt

Name _____

▶ **Write in what section of the library you would find each item listed below. Choose from the choices at the right.**

1. a fairy tale

_____

2. a book on the solar system

_____

3. an atlas or almanac

_____

Fiction

Nonfiction

Reference

4. a book about dinosaurs

_____

5. a newspaper or magazine

_____

6. an encyclopedia

_____

7. a book about children who sell dreams

_____

▶ **Choose the reference source where you would find each item.**

newspaper	encyclopedia	phone book

8. an advertisement for a pet business _____

9. a friend's telephone number _____

10. information about guinea pigs _____

TRY THIS! Write five reasons to use a library's card catalog or reference sources.

Harcourt

Name _____

▶ **The sentences below tell how to write a story, but they are not in the right order. On the lines, write the sentences in the correct order and circle the time-order words.**

- Then figure out the time—past, present, or future.
- As you reread, look for misspellings and grammar errors.
- So, the last thing you do is revise it.
- There is much to think about when you begin to write a story.
- Then decide what happens to the main character.
- The first thing you decide is where the story will take place.
- When you finish writing your first draft, reread your story.
- After you decide on a place and time, think about the main character.

1. _____

2. _____

3. _____

4. _____

   _____

5. _____

6. _____

7. _____

8. _____

TRY THIS! Choose a page in a history or social studies book. Find time-order words. Use each one in a sentence.

Harcourt

Name _____

▶ **If the words form a sentence, write** *sentence*. **If they do not, think of words to make the sentence complete. Then write the new sentence.**

1. Buster and Arthur.

_____

2. Looked it up in the dictionary.

_____

3. Found out something new.

_____

4. Were they surprised?

_____

5. The tall librarian.

_____

▶ **Rewrite each group of words in the correct order to form a sentence that makes sense. Begin and end each sentence correctly.**

6. dinosaurs my friend wrote about.

_____

7. would my story read you?

_____

8. the title my sister does not like.

_____

9. when the stories due are?

_____

10. the story like will teacher my.

_____

Name _____

▶ **Write a Spelling Word from the box to complete each sentence.**

camp   best
send   hand

1. I like to _____ under the stars.

2. Kurt hurt his _____.

3. Wendy will _____ the letter.

4. Charlene is the _____ runner.

▶ **Write these Spelling Words in alphabetical order.**

felt   next   last   went

5. _____   **7.** _____

6. _____   **8.** _____

Handwriting Tip: When you join *a* to another letter, complete the down stroke first. Write these words.

_____

am

9. past _____   **10.** stand _____

SCHOOL-HOME CONNECTION Ask your child to tell you about his or her day. After each sentence, take note of the words that have short a and short e, such as *backpack* and *pen*. Make a list of these words, and review them with your child.

Harcourt

Name _____

▶ **Complete each sentence with a word from the box.**

| magnets | sorting | ignore | attract | decorated | connected |

1. I will see if these

_____ stick
to the chains on
the swings.

2. Yes! They

_____.

3. These bread crumbs will

_____ those pretty birds.

4. I thought this dog would

_____ me, but
he's very friendly!

5. _____ these leaves by
size will be fun.

6. Look at how I've

_____ this box!

▶ **Use Vocabulary Words to complete this sentence.**

7–8. If you want to _____ friends, you can't _____ people.

SCHOOL-HOME CONNECTION With your child, talk about a
neighborhood event. As you talk, try to use at least two of the
Vocabulary Words.

Hidden Surprises **11**

Harcourt

Name _____

Skill Reminder A prefix is a small word part at the beginning of a word. A suffix is a small word part at the end of a word.

▶ In each advertisement, find the three words with prefixes or suffixes. Then write each word, its prefix or suffix, and the word's meaning.

Prefix	Suffix	Meaning
dis-		opposite of; not
non-		not
over-		too much
	-able	able to; being
	-tion, -ion	the act of

Are you ready for a day of nonstop fun? If so, come to the fair. We promise great games without interruption, and great food. You will not disagree.

1. _____

2. _____

3. _____

Magnets for Sale!
Usable on refrigerators or just for a magnet collection! We do not overcharge.

4. _____

5. _____

6. _____

Do you dislike a mess?
Is your room overfilled with boxes of junk? Try our dependable cleaning service.

7. _____

_____

8. _____

_____

9. _____

_____

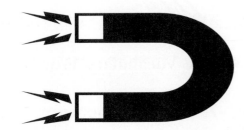

Harcourt

Name _____

▶ Complete this story map as you read "Marta's Magnets." List only the most important events.

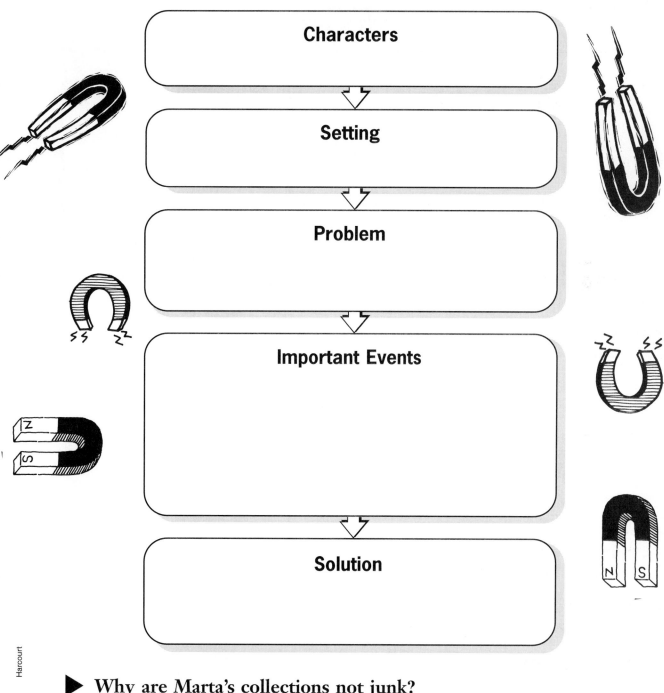

Characters

Setting

Problem

Important Events

Solution

Harcourt

▶ Why are Marta's collections not junk?

_____

_____

_____

Name _____

▶ **Write two word parts or shorter words found within
each word.**

1. talking _____ _____

2. rainfall _____ _____

3. reread _____ _____

4. nonstop _____ _____

5. unclear _____ _____

6. fixable _____ _____

7. disagree _____ _____

8. direction _____ _____

9. sunflower _____ _____

10. townhouse _____ _____

TRY THIS! Look through a science book for words you are not familiar with. Make a list of these words. Then use word identification strategies to figure out how to pronounce these words.

Harcourt

Name _____

▶ **Read the words in the magnets. Place each word in the related group of words below.**

collection   disfavor   otherwise   appearance

1. collect
collector

_____

2. other
another

_____

3. favor
favorite

_____

4. appear
disappear

_____

▶ **Read each sentence. Then write the correct definition of the underlined word on the line.**

5. Marta had a <u>collection</u> for everything.
   a. answer to a problem   **b.** group of things kept together

_____

6. The <u>appearance</u> of her room was not always neat.
   a. way something looks   **b.** painted wall

_____

7. This put her in <u>disfavor</u> with her sister.
   a. being happy   **b.** being disapproved of

_____

8. Marta must clean up. <u>Otherwise</u>, Rosa will complain.
   a. anyway   **b.** if not

_____

Name _____

► After each sentence, write *statement* or *question* to tell
what kind of sentence it is.

1. Do you have my banana magnet?

_____

2. I put it on the refrigerator.

_____

3. I like your collection of magnets.

_____

4. Can you reach that frog magnet?

_____

► Add the correct end mark to each sentence.

5. Marta's magnets are in a box __

6. Where did she get this magnet __

7. She found that one in a science kit __

8. Doesn't it look like a small horseshoe __

► Write a question about the magnets. Then write a statement to
answer the question.

9. _____

_____

10. _____

_____

16 Hidden Surprises

SCHOOL-HOME CONNECTION Look through a newspaper
with your child. Choose four headlines to rewrite into complete
statements or questions. Add correct end marks.

Harcourt

Name _____

▶ **Write Spelling Words from the box to complete the sentences.**

rocks	lunch	truck	jump

After we eat **(1)** _____ in the park, we skip and

(2) _____ over the **(3)** _____. Then,

we buy treats from the ice-cream **(4)** _____.

▶ **Write the Spelling Word from the box that fits each shape.**

gift	thing	pond	from

5.

6.

7.

8.

Handwriting Tip: Do not loop an *i,* or it might look like an *l.*
Write these words.

9. inch _____ **10.** fish _____

SCHOOL-HOME CONNECTION On billboards, in ads, and on
food boxes, look for words with short *i, o,* and *u,* such as *milk,*
box, and *mug.* Make lists and review the words with your child.

Hidden Surprises

Name _____

▶ **Complete each sentence with a word from the box.**

medals	harmonica	counselor
poisonous	practiced	cheered

1. Don't worry about winning any

_____.

Just have fun!

4. Have you

_____

those camp songs
I taught you?

2. Watch out for the

_____ snakes

shown in this book.

5. You might enjoy playing

this _____.

3. As a camp

_____,

I'll make sure
everyone has fun.

6. If you get sad, just remember

how everyone _____
when you made that home run.

▶ **Use Vocabulary Words to complete this question and answer.**

7. Question: Who will win the most _____?

8. Answer: It will be someone who _____!

 TRY THIS! Be on the lookout for people who deserve medals! They might be other students, or they might be people in the news. Write about one of them. Try to use at least two of the Vocabulary Words.

Harcourt

Name _____

Skill Reminder **When you add a prefix or suffix to a word, the meaning of the word changes.**

Prefix	Meaning
dis-	opposite of
non-	not
over-	too much

Suffix	Meaning
-able	able to; being
-tion	the act of
-ion	the act of

▶ **Add a prefix or suffix to each base word. Then use the new word in a sentence.**

1. approve _____

_____

2. sleep _____

_____

3. agree _____

_____

4. perfect _____

_____

5. due _____

_____

6. stick _____

_____

7. read _____

_____

8. collect _____

_____

Name _____

Skill Reminder The card catalog or a computer
database lists every book in the library or media center.

▶ Ronald Morgan wants to find out about Native
American ceremonies for a camp show. Use the
following cards from a library card catalog to answer these questions.

1. Which card from the card catalog
is a title card?

_____

2. Which card from the card catalog
is an author card?

_____

3. Which card from the card catalog
is a subject card?

_____

4. What is the call number for the title?

_____

5. Who is the author of the book?

_____

6. What is the title of the book?

_____

7. What other information can you
find on the cards?

_____

_____

8. What kind of information would you expect to find in the book?

_____

_____

Card A

> **J394.268** Ancona, George
> Anc
>
> *Powwow*
> Harcourt, Inc. (1993)   45 p. illus
> See also Native Americans;
> Indian ceremonies

Card B

> **J394.268** *Powwow*
> Anc
>
> Ancona, George
> *Powwow*
> Harcourt, Inc. (1993)   45 p. illus
> See also Native Americans; Indian ceremonies

Card C

> **J394.268** Native American Ceremonies
> Anc
>
> Ancona, George
> *Powwow*
> Harcourt, Inc. (1993)   45 p. illus
> See also Native Americans; Indian ceremonies

SCHOOL-HOME CONNECTION With your child, visit a library or media
center. Have the librarian show you how to use the card catalog and a
computer database. Then, look for an interesting book.

Harcourt

Name _____

▶ As you read "Ronald Morgan Goes to Camp,"
complete the prediction web below. After reading,
fill in what actually happens.

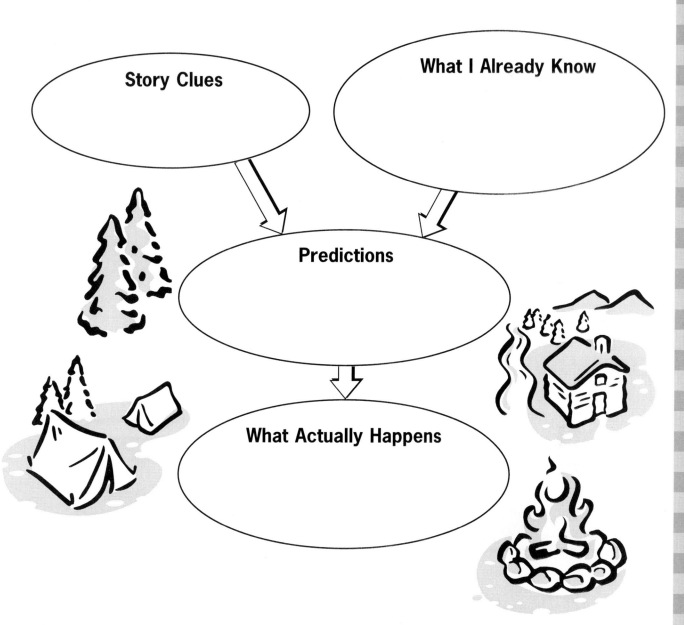

Story Clues

What I Already Know

Predictions

What Actually Happens

▶ How does Ronald Morgan feel about himself at the end of the story?
Why?

_____

_____

_____

Harcourt

Name _____

▶ **Read the passage. Then fill in the chart.**

Ronald was walking back to his tent. He wondered why he was trying to be a great camper. Everyone else was good at something. Just then Ronald noticed some footprints. He decided to follow them.

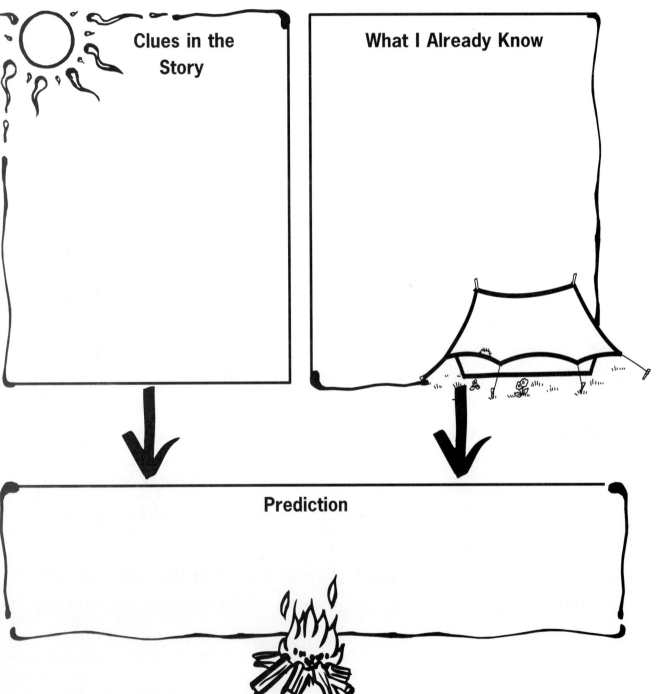

Clues in the Story

What I Already Know

Prediction

Harcourt

SCHOOL-HOME CONNECTION With your child, find a picture and begin a story about the picture. Ask a family member to make a prediction about the ending of your story. Then work together to finish it.

Name _____

▶ **Read the passage and then answer the questions.**
Fill in the oval next to your choice.

Ronald and his friends decide to have a talent show. He says, "I want everyone to be in the show, but one act should be the most exciting." Ronald looks at his harmonica.

"I could sing," says Jan.

"That's great," says Ronald, "but we need something even more exciting."

"I can read a poem," says Michael.

Ronald says, "Fine. What else?"

Francine announces, "I know how to juggle."

1 Who do you predict will speak next?

⬭ Jan

⬭ Ronald

⬭ Michael

⬭ Francine

2 On what do you base your prediction?

⬭ Ronald has been speaking after each person does.

⬭ Ronald wants to say he plays the harmonica.

⬭ No one else has any ideas.

⬭ Francine wants Ronald to be in charge of the show.

3 What do you predict will happen next?

⬭ Ronald will cancel the talent show.

⬭ Ronald will listen to Michael's poem.

⬭ Ronald will say they need something more exciting.

⬭ Ronald will try to get Jan to dance instead of sing.

4 What act might Ronald think would be exciting?

⬭ a comedy act

⬭ baton twirling

⬭ showing a bug collection

⬭ Ronald playing the harmonica

Harcourt

Name _____

▶ Each tent is used to store things that go together.
Read the words on the pictures below. Then write the
words in the groups where they belong.

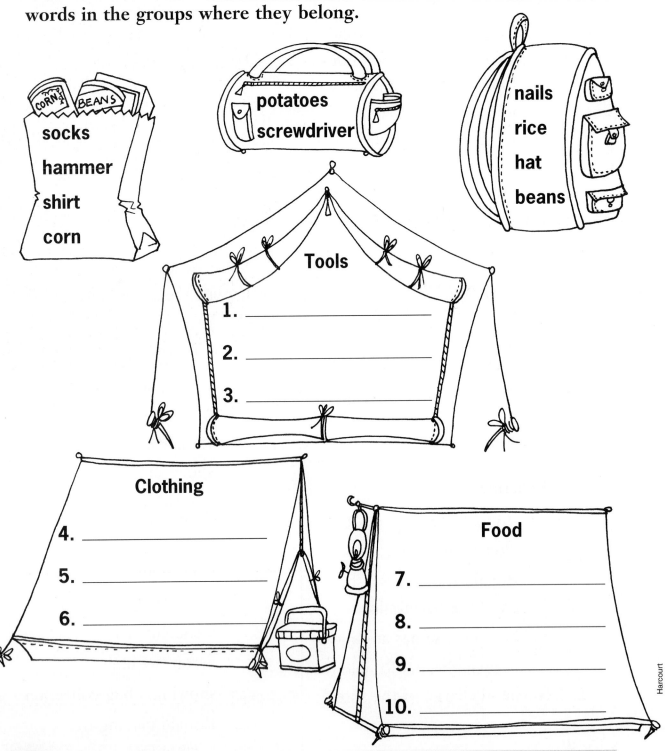

CORN BEANS

socks

hammer

shirt

corn

potatoes
screwdriver

nails

rice

hat

beans

Tools

1. _____

2. _____

3. _____

Clothing

4. _____

5. _____

6. _____

Food

7. _____

8. _____

9. _____

10. _____

TRY THIS! Imagine that you are packing for camp. You need supplies for hiking, swimming, sleeping, and writing letters home. Make lists of what you will bring. Give each list a different heading.

Harcourt

Name _____

Ronald Morgan
Goes to Camp

**Grammar:
Commands and
Exclamations**

▶ **Write *command* or *exclamation* to tell what kind of
sentence each is. Add the correct end
mark to each sentence.**

1. Wow, those mountains are high___

_____

2. What a warm night it is___

_____

3. Look at the stars overhead___

_____

4. How beautiful it is here___

_____

5. Play your harmonica, Ronald___ _____

6. Tell me a scary story___ _____

▶ **Use each word in parentheses ( ) in a complete sentence.
For C, write a command. For E, write an exclamation.**

7. (owl) C: _____

8. (yikes) E: _____

9. (run) E: _____

10. (watch) C: _____

 TRY THIS! On a separate sheet of paper, write a skit based on the story.
Include all four types of sentences in your skit.

Harcourt

Name _____

▶ **Write the Spelling Word that best completes
each sentence.**

grade	reach	name	trail

1. For the field trip for third _____, Ms. Mason's class went
on a hike.

2. The hike was on a winding dirt _____.

3. The class was trying to _____ a place to rent boats.

4. The _____ of the place was Kent Lake Boat Rentals.

▶ **Write the Spelling Word from the box that goes with each clue.**

pail	lake	these	raise

5. not those   _____

6. rhymes with *days* _____

7. sounds like *pale* _____

8. is full of water   _____

Handwriting Tip: Loop an *e* so it does not look like an *i*.
Write these words.

_____

_____ℓ_____

9. leave _____   **10.** dream _____

Harcourt

26 Hidden Surprises

SCHOOL-HOME CONNECTION Ask your child for something he or she
has written. Look it over for words with long a, as in *day*, and long e, as
in *eat*. Point out the words to your child, and read them aloud together.

Name _____

▶ **Finish each sentence with a word from the box.**

aimed	noticed	pretended
professional	applauded	familiar

1. If you've played a game many times, it is

a _____ game to you.

2. If you acted as if you were a famous

basketball player, you _____.

3. If you clapped for the winning team,

you _____.

4. If you saw a player make a great basket,

you _____ it.

5. If you want to have a job playing basketball when

you grow up, you want to be a _____ player.

6. If you tossed the ball toward the basket, you _____ it.

▶ **Use a Vocabulary Word to fill in each blank.**

7. saw = _____   **9.** pointed at = _____

8. clapped = _____   **10.** acted = _____

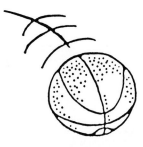

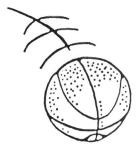

SCHOOL-HOME CONNECTION Help your child write a letter
to another family member, using as many of the Vocabulary
Words as possible.

Harcourt

Name _____

Skill Reminder Readers use story information and what they already know to predict outcomes.

▶ After you read the passage, fill in the chart. Predict what will happen next.

    The day of the big game was here. Both teams were looking forward to a great match. The problem was the weather. It was cloudy and cold. The forecast was for rain—the same forecast as for the past two days. But it hadn't rained until evening each day. There were cumulus clouds in the sky, fluffy clouds that meant the possibility of a thunderstorm that might not last all day. The game would be played outside, starting at 3:00 P.M. But would the weather hold?

What I Already Know

Clues in the Story

Prediction

SCHOOL-HOME CONNECTION With your child, go outside and look at the clouds. Make a prediction about the weather.

Harcourt

Name _____

▶ Before you read "Allie's Basketball Dream," write your predictions in the chart below. After you read the story, write what actually happens. Remember to tell only the main events.

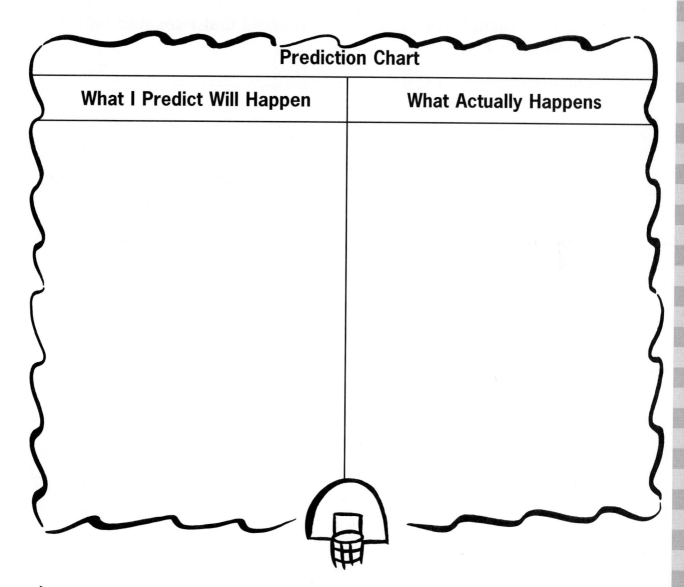

Prediction Chart

What I Predict Will Happen	What Actually Happens

▶ Why do you think Allie is successful at making a basket?

_____

_____

_____

Harcourt

Name _____

▶ **Choose the correct meaning for each underlined word, and write it on the line. Then write a sentence using the other meaning of the word.**

1. The basketball players <u>wave</u> to the fans after they win the game.

move the hand back and forth in a greeting   **a liquid that rises and falls**

meaning: _____

sentence: _____

2. The audience waves <u>back</u> at the players.

in return   **the part of the body that is on the side opposite the chest**

meaning: _____

sentence: _____

3. The color of the team's uniforms was <u>light</u> blue.

not heavy   **pale**

meaning: _____

sentence: _____

4. A loud cheer <u>rose</u> from the stands as Allie scored.

a type of flower   **came up**

meaning: _____

sentence: _____

5. The dog's loud <u>bark</u> greeted Allie when she got home.

the short, quick cry of a dog   **part of a tree**

meaning: _____

sentence: _____

TRY THIS! For each of these multiple-meaning words, write two sentences, each with a different meaning: *bank, hide, sharp, turn, beam.*

Harcourt

Name _____

▶ **Match each word listed below with a word on a basketball to make a compound word. Write the compound word on the line.**

1. basket _____

2. side _____

3. bull _____

4. skate _____

5. sun _____

6. play _____

7. thunder _____

8. news _____

9. sweat _____

10. lip _____

frog

paper

stick

storm

ground

shine

board

shine

shirt

ball

walk

 TRY THIS!

Write five sentences using some of the new words that you just made.

Harcourt

Name _____

▶ **Draw one line under each subject.**
Draw two lines under each predicate.

1. Allie's friends played in the park.

2. One small girl jumped rope.

3. Julio whizzed by on his skateboard.

4. The park is a wonderful place.

5. Allie feels happy there.

▶ **Add a subject or a predicate to complete each sentence.**

6. The basketball _____.

7. _____ played with a volleyball.

8. _____ watched the game.

9. Some boys _____.

10. _____ cheered for Allie.

 TRY THIS! Write three statements about playing a game. Draw one line under the subjects. Draw two lines under the predicates. Read your sentences to a partner, and ask what the subject and the predicate of each sentence is.

Harcourt

Name _____

▶ **Write the Spelling Words from the box that best complete the sentences.**

while	bright	window	time

(1) _____ I was looking out the **(2)** _____ ,

I thought about a day last summer. The day was **(3)** _____

and sunny. What a good **(4)** _____ we had that day!

▶ **Unscramble the underlined words, and write the correct Spelling Word on the line.**

show	whole	tight	close

5. I will <u>whos</u> you how to play. _____

6. My shoes feel too <u>htigt</u> . _____

7. That was so <u>solce</u> ! _____

8. Let's practice the <u>helow</u> afternoon. _____

Handwriting Tip: When you join an *o* to another letter, keep the joining stroke high so it doesn't look like an *a*. Write these words.

9. follow _____ **10.** stone _____

SCHOOL-HOME CONNECTION With your child, make lists of words that rhyme with *might* (*right, tight, recite*) and with *show* (*bow, low, below*).

Hidden Surprises **33**

Harcourt

▶ **Finish this letter. Use words from the box to complete the sentences.**

Olympic Games		**meters**	**furiously**
talent	**complained**	**respect**	**championships**

Dear Aunt Joan,

This event is so exciting! I'm happy to be here with all the other swimmers.

This afternoon, I was swimming as hard as I could to win the race. With only a few **(1)** _____ to go, I swallowed a mouthful of water. I lost that race, but the

(2) _____ are not over yet.

Even though I **(3)** _____ the other swimmers, I think I have a good chance to win a medal.

The other swimmers have **(4)** _____,

that's for sure. Still, one of them **(5)** _____

yesterday about a sore muscle. That can even happen to a

swimmer in the **(6)** _____!

You know how **(7)** _____ I have been practicing. I want to win! Wish me luck.

Your niece,
Cindy

TRY THIS! Write a letter to a friend or relative telling about something you'd like to win. Use some of the Vocabulary Words in your letter.

Name _____

Skill Reminder When you read a story, you think about what might happen next. This is called making predictions.

▶ Read this beginning of a magazine article, and answer the questions.

Olympic Games—Past to Present

The Olympics began in ancient Greece. They were held every four years. Early Olympic Games included competitions in physical activities such as running and weightlifting and in music, speaking, and drama as well.

1. What do you think the rest of this article will be about?

_____

2. Why did you make this prediction?

_____

3. What kinds of details do you think might be in this article?

_____

4. Why do you think this?

_____

5. Is this the kind of article you would enjoy reading? Why or why not?

_____

6. Do you think the rest of this article will tell about one athlete?

_____

7. Do you think every Olympic Game event will be mentioned? Explain.

_____

8. How do you think the article will end?

_____

Harcourt

Name _____

Skill Reminder Use these word identification strategies:

- **Look for syllable patterns and spelling patterns.**
- **Look for word parts or shorter words.**
- **Blend consonant sounds with vowel sounds.**
- **Look for clues to meaning in nearby words.**

▶ **Read the paragraph. Then write how you figured out the pronunciation of each underlined word.**

Jenna knew that being an <u>athlete</u> means being in pain sometimes. Even though she had done a complete and <u>proper</u> <u>workout</u>, her body was <u>demanding</u> that she rest. But she had won the <u>national</u> <u>championships</u>, and she wasn't going to let a little pain stop her <u>progress</u>. She headed for the showers. Maybe the <u>warmth</u> of the water would ease her pain.

1. athlete _____

2. proper _____

_____

3. workout _____

4. demanding _____

_____

5. national _____

6. championships _____

_____

7. progress _____

8. warmth _____

_____

Harcourt

Name _____

▶ Read the first two pages of "Water Woman." Then complete the first two columns of this chart. After you finish reading, complete the third column.

K	W	L
What I Know	**What I Want to Know**	**What I Learned**

▶ What words would you use to describe Amy Van Dyken? Give reasons from the story for your answer.

_____

_____

_____

Harcourt

Name _____

▶ **Read the descriptions of the books below. Then tell whether each book is fiction or nonfiction and how you know.**

1. a book about the life of a famous Olympic swimmer

_____

_____

2. a book that shows diagrams of swimming strokes

_____

_____

3. an adventure book about a made-up person who swims the Atlantic Ocean

_____

_____

4. a book that describes Colorado State University

_____

_____

5. a book about mermaids

_____

_____

_____

6. a book about asthma

_____

_____

7. a travel guide showing the best roads in the southern states

_____

_____

8. a book about third-grade boys who can fly like birds

_____

_____

Harcourt

Name _____

▶ **Write the type of nonfiction that best matches each description. Choose from the types in the box. You may use each type more than once.**

| news story | newsletter | magazine article |
| how-to article | informational book | |

1. It has an article about a neighborhood meeting.

   _____

2. It tells what steps to take in order to become a champion.

   _____

3. It is divided into sections with headings about the Olympics.

   _____

4. It has a headline saying that Amy won four gold medals.

   _____

5. It has news about Colorado State University.

   _____

6. One of the subheadings in the article is about events at the Olympic Games.

   _____

7. It tells how to become a better swimmer.

   _____

8. It tells who Amy is, what she did, and when she did it.

   _____

▶ **Write the purpose for reading each type of nonfiction.**

9. Why would Amy have read her college newsletter?

   _____

10. Why would someone read Amy's biography?

   _____

Name _____

▶ **Complete each sentence or pair of sentences by writing the same word in each blank. Choose from the words in the box.**

| flight | stand | meet | pool | fans | back | second | feet |

1. The _____ watched from the bleachers. They

   used _____ to keep cool.

2. Brett and Jan had to _____ their money. Then they bought

   tickets to swim in the _____.

3. Rosie's _____ hurt terribly. She had to go _____ home.

4. We had to _____ in the sun for hours. Finally, we

   couldn't _____ the heat any longer.

5. From the bottom of her _____ to the top of

   her head, Amy is four _____ tall.

6. Amy got out of breath running up the _____ of stairs at the

   airport. Luckily, she was on time for her _____.

7. The swimmer who came in _____ lost by less than one _____.

8. Amy ran to _____ her teammates. She didn't want to be late

   for the _____.

TRY THIS! Write sentences, using the words *left*, *over*, and *well*.

40 Hidden Surprises

Harcourt

Name _____

▶ **Underline each compound subject once and each compound predicate twice. Then write** *compound subject* **or** *compound predicate* **to tell what each sentence has.**

1. Amy and her coach came up with a plan. _____

2. Amy's skill and speed made her a star. _____

3. She worked hard and succeeded. _____

4. Amy won a medal and was named swimmer of the year.

_____

5. Amy's fans and fellow athletes look up to her. _____

6. A champion has courage and never gives up. _____

▶ **Rewrite each sentence. Place commas where they are needed. Then underline each compound subject once and each compound predicate twice.**

7. Your goggles towel and cap are on the bench.

_____

8. The girl jumps splashes and paddles around.

_____

9. Parents friends and fans fill the stands.

_____

10. The swimmers stretch warm up and get ready.

_____

TRY THIS! Write two sentences about swimming. Give one sentence a compound subject. Give the other sentence a compound predicate.

Harcourt

Name _____

▶ **Write the Spelling Word that best completes each sentence.**

least	burst	artist	fast

Last year, she was the **(1)** _____ likely to win, but look at her this year! She'll need a real **(2)** _____ of speed to get ahead. Her practice time was so **(3)** _____ that I'm sure she'll win. I'd like to hire an **(4)** _____ to paint this moment.

▶ **Use these Spelling Words and the clues below to complete the puzzle.**

strike	stick	strip	student

Down

5. pupil
6. pole

Across

7. band
8. hit

Handwriting Tip: When writing *st*, be sure the *t* does not look like an *l*. Write these words.

9. just _____   **10.** almost _____

SCHOOL-HOME CONNECTION With your child, look around your home for items whose names have the consonant blend *st*, such as *stairs*, *toaster*, and *footstool*.

Harcourt

Name Samuel Marsh

▶ Read each group of words on the bulletin board, and write the word from the box that goes best with each group.

department	obeys	commands
audience	expression	accident

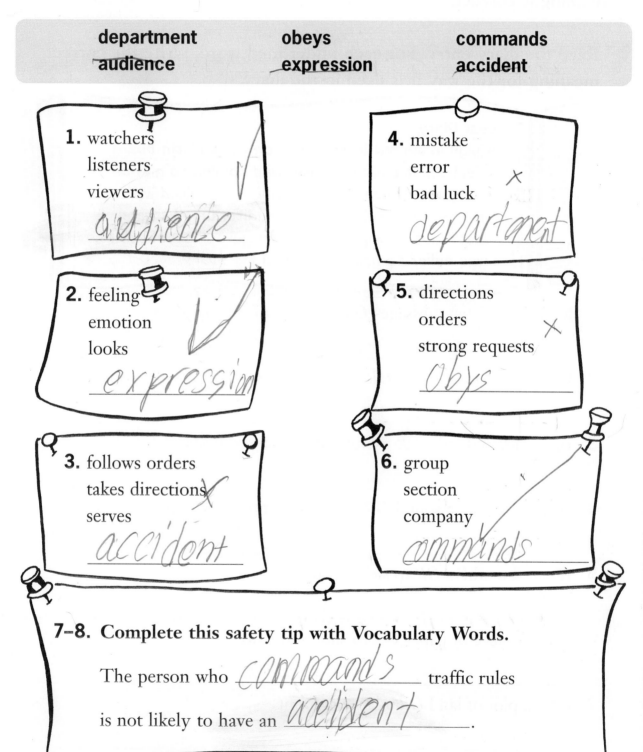

1. watchers
listeners
viewers
audience ✓

2. feeling
emotion
looks
expression ✓

3. follows orders
takes directions ✗
serves
accident

4. mistake
error
bad luck ✗
department

5. directions
orders
strong requests ✗
obys

6. group
section
company
commands

7–8. Complete this safety tip with Vocabulary Words.

The person who _commands_ traffic rules

is not likely to have an _accident_ .

Harcourt

Name _____

Skill Reminder **Many words have more than one
meaning. Use other words in the sentence to figure out which
meaning is correct.**

▶ **Read the diary entry. For each underlined word, write the correct
meaning for the way it is used in the diary.**

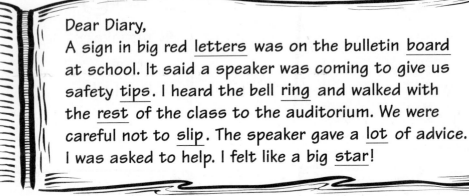

Dear Diary,
A sign in big red <u>letters</u> was on the bulletin <u>board</u>
at school. It said a speaker was coming to give us
safety <u>tips</u>. I heard the bell <u>ring</u> and walked with
the <u>rest</u> of the class to the auditorium. We were
careful not to <u>slip</u>. The speaker gave a <u>lot</u> of advice.
I was asked to help. I felt like a big <u>star</u>!

1. letters—written messages *OR* symbols of the alphabet

_____

2. board—a slab of wood *OR* flat surface used for posting notices

_____

3. tips—pointed ends *OR* useful hints or suggestions

_____

4. ring—to make a sound *OR* jewelry worn on the finger

_____

5. rest—the others *OR* to sleep or relax

_____

6. slip—a piece of paper *OR* to slide suddenly

_____

7. lot—a plot of land *OR* a large amount

_____

8. star—a well-known actor *OR* a light shining in the sky

_____

Harcourt

Name _____

► Complete this sequence chart as you read "Officer
Buckle and Gloria."

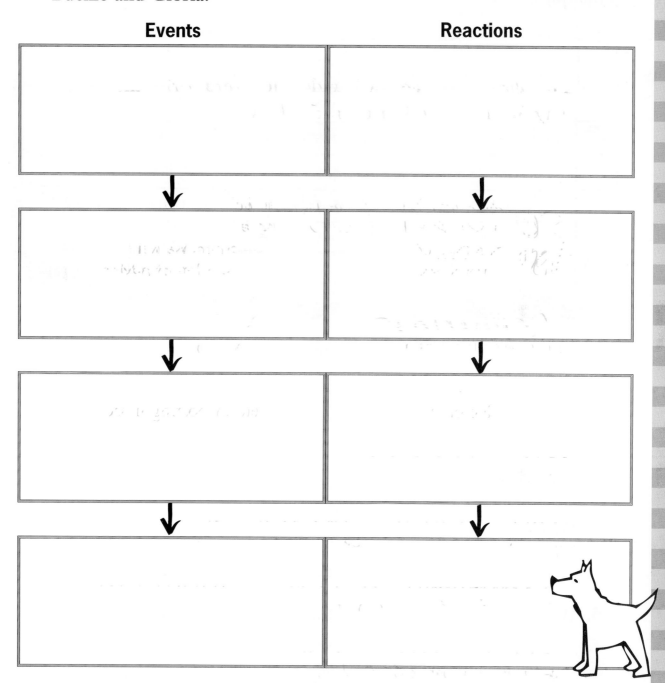

Events	Reactions

► Name five safety tips that Officer Buckle mentioned.

_____

_____

_____

Harcourt

Name _____

▶ **Read the following passage. Then answer
the questions.**

> Matt and Kurtis were in front of Matt's house. They had decided to bike over to Kurtis's house. As they reached for their helmets, Matt noticed something was wrong with his. "Oh no," he said, "the strap's broken. I won't be able to go."
>
> Kurtis said, "My house is only two blocks away. You don't need your helmet." Matt thought about what he should do.

1. Who are the characters in the story? _____

2. What is the setting of the story? _____

3. What is Matt's problem? _____

_____

4. Why does Kurtis say Matt doesn't need his helmet? _____

_____

5. Why do you think Matt has to think about what to do? _____

_____

6. How do you think Matt will solve his problem? _____

_____

TRY THIS! Work with a partner. Think of a safety rule not mentioned in "Officer Buckle and Gloria." Write it on a poster and share it with the class.

Harcourt

Name _____

▶ **Read the passage and then answer the questions.**
Fill in the oval next to your choice.

Jessica and her dad were eating their picnic lunch. Suddenly they heard yelping coming from the woods. Dad and Jessica got to their feet and started to run toward the spot where they thought they heard the sound. Dad told Jessica to be careful and not to run ahead of him. After a few minutes they reached the spot. Trapped in a large hole was a very scared dog. Jessica and her dad got a rope and pulled the dog to safety.

1 Where does the story take place?

- ⬭ school
- ⬭ a meadow
- ⬭ near the woods
- ⬭ on vacation

2 Who are the characters?

- ⬭ Jessica
- ⬭ Jessica's dad
- ⬭ a scared dog
- ⬭ Jessica, Jessica's dad, and a scared dog

3 What is the problem?

- ⬭ There is not enough food.
- ⬭ There is a dog in trouble in the woods.
- ⬭ Jessica's dad can't run fast.
- ⬭ The dog is very big.

4 What happens first?

- ⬭ Jessica saves the dog.
- ⬭ Jessica and her dad run.
- ⬭ Jessica and her dad were eating their lunch.
- ⬭ Jessica and her dad get a rope.

5 What safety advice does Jessica's dad give her?

- ⬭ not to run too fast
- ⬭ not to touch the dog
- ⬭ not to run ahead of him
- ⬭ to call for help

6 What is the solution?

- ⬭ Jessica runs slowly.
- ⬭ Jessica calls for help.
- ⬭ Jessica and her dad run.
- ⬭ Jessica and her dad use a rope to save the dog.

Harcourt

Name _____

► **Officer Buckle wrote all these notes to himself, but then he forgot what the abbreviations mean. Help him by writing each note out in full.**

1. On Tues., Jan. 31, go to Elm Ave.

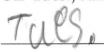 

Tues. Jan 19 Avenue

2. On Sat., Feb. 4, see Dr. Vega.

saterday feb DR

3. On Fri., Mar. 3, visit Main St.

fridymar

4. Go to Rock Rd. on Mon.

Rd mon

5. See Mr. Soto about soccer game on Sun.

mr Soto game

6. Get two ft. of rope at store on Third Ave.

Trftd Ave

7. Go to Walnut Dr. for party.

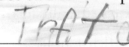 

Drva party

8. Go to store on Flores Rd. on Wed.

 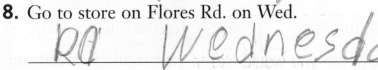

Rd Wednesday

TRY THIS!

Make a list of what you plan to do next week and when you plan to do it. Use as many abbreviations as you can.

Harcourt

Name _Samuel M_

▶ **Underline the correct joining word in each
compound sentence.**

1. Officer Buckle's talk was dull, (**and** / but) the children were bored.

2. He tried to be exciting, (and / **but**) the students just yawned.

3. Then Gloria acted silly, (**and** / but) everyone began to laugh.

4. Gloria seemed to obey, (and / **but**) she really acted silly.

▶ **Join each pair of sentences with a comma, followed by
and or *but*. Write the compound sentences on the
lines below.**

5. We had fun. We learned a lot. (**and**)

    we learned a lot

6. Safety rules may seem boring. They are important. (**but**)

    safety we was said

7. Gloria was just a dog. She was very smart. (**but**)

    officer Buckle was smart to

8. Officer Buckle learned the truth. It surprised him. (**and**)

    the dog was doing good

9. Officer Buckle tried hard. Gloria was the star. (**but**)

    the dog have a star to

10. Now he works with Gloria. They are good buddies. (**and**)

    They works good tems

**TRY
THIS!** Think of a famous person you would like to visit your school. Tell
why you would like to see that person. Use at least two compound
sentences in your explanation. Share it with a friend.

Harcourt

Name _____

▶ **Write the Spelling Word from the box that best completes each sentence.**

known	laugh	wrong	wrap	knocked	wreck

Brad **(1)** _____ on his friend Heather's door one morning.

"I wish I had **(2)** _____ you were coming," said Heather.

"My room is just a **(3)** _____! Let's go to the park to play."

"I guess I was **(4)** _____ not to call first," said Brad. "The

park sounds fine. Let's **(5)** _____ up some sandwiches and an

apple for the officer's horse. We can take the dogs,

tell some jokes, and have a good **(6)** _____."

▶ **Write the Spelling Word that goes with each clue.**

written	sphere	writer	wrench

7. ball _____

8. author _____

9. a tool _____

10. not spoken _____

Handwriting Tip: When writing an *h*, make sure it is open and not closed, so it does not look like a *b*. Write these words.

h

11. laugh _____

12. sphere _____

SCHOOL-HOME CONNECTION With your child, make up sentences using the Spelling Words and other words that have *kn, wr, gh,* and *ph,* such as *knight, wreath, cough,* and *telephone.*

Harcourt

Name _Samuel_

▶ On the lines below, write the word from the box that completes each sentence.

trained	wise	message	patiently	litter	eager

Pick up the **(1)** _message_ on the beach. Then write a **(2)** _litter_ in the local newspaper asking for the community to help. A **(3)** _trained_ dog will fetch and keep you company as you work. Don't pick up all the trash by yourself. Sit and wait **(4)** _wise_ for others to come. A **(5)** _litter_ teacher may let an **(6)** _eager_ student organize a time to clean the beach.

▶ Complete the sentence with two Vocabulary Words.

7–8. A person who is _____ might be in a hurry, but a calm person waits _____.

SCHOOL-HOME CONNECTION With your child, write a list of animal facts. Use as many of the Vocabulary Words as possible.

Harcourt

Name _____

Skill Reminder | **All stories have a setting, characters, a problem, events, and a solution.**

► Write the answers to the questions below. Tell about the setting, characters, problem, important events, and solution for the story "Turtle Bay."

1. Who are the characters in the story?

_____

2. What is the setting of this story? _____

3. What is the problem? _____

_____

4. What are the important events in the story? _____

_____

_____

5. How is the problem solved? _____

_____

6. How do you know the eggs hatched? _____

7. What else could people do to make the beach safe for the turtles?

_____

8. What about the story led you to think it was about turtles? _____

_____

Harcourt

Name _____

▶ As you read "Turtle Bay," complete the story map below. List only the most important events.

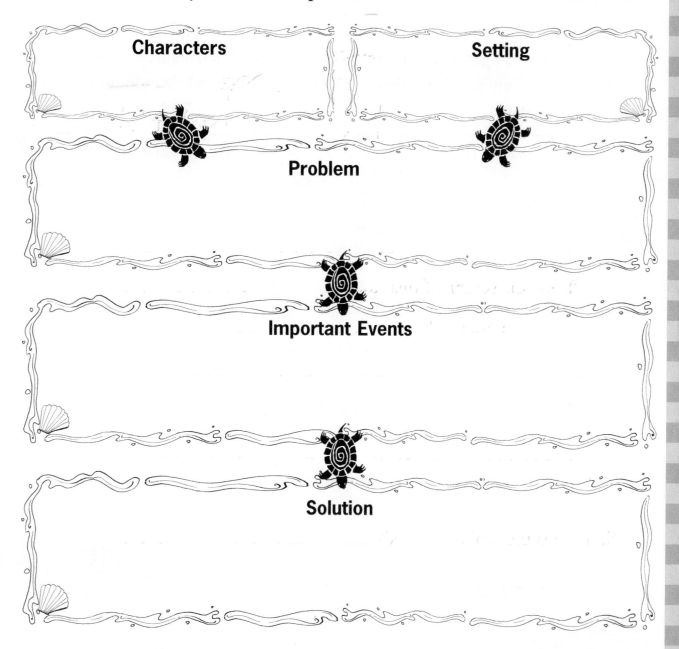

Characters

Setting

Problem

Important Events

Solution

▶ Answer the following questions.

1. How do the children feel at the beginning of the story?

_____

2. How do they feel at the end of the story?

_____

Harcourt

Name _____

▶ **Read the paragraph about Jiro-San. What conclusions can you draw about him? Complete the chart below.**

Jiro-San often sits on a rock, looking at the water and listening. He listens for messages from the wind. He looks for his friends, and he tries to make things safe for them. Jiro-San's friends include whales, dolphins, fish, and sea turtles.

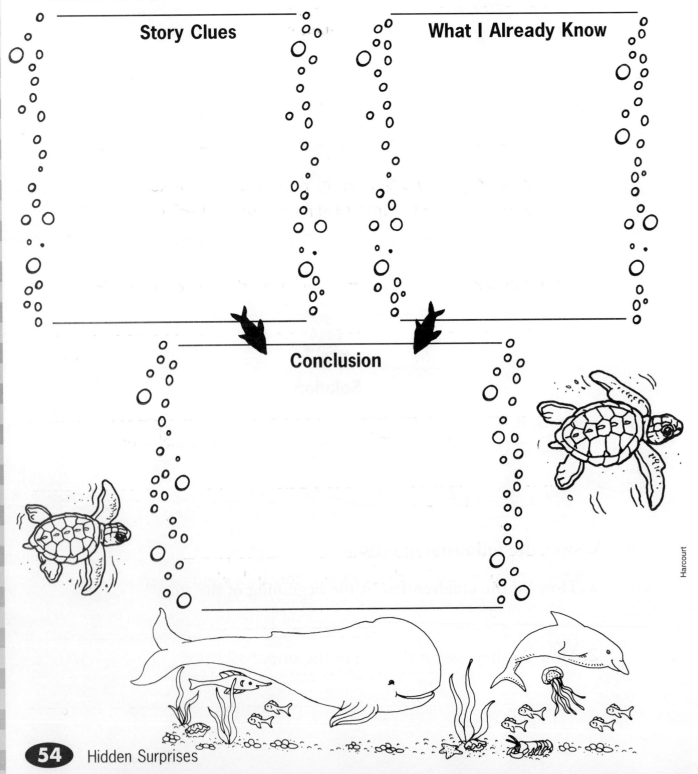

Story Clues

What I Already Know

Conclusion

Harcourt

Name _____

▶ **Read each paragraph. Then answer the questions.**

Taro watches Jiro-San and wonders what secrets he has. Taro helps Jiro-San sweep the beach, not knowing why they are doing it.

1. What conclusions can you draw about Taro? _____

 _____

2. What clues in the paragraph helped you draw your conclusion?

_____

 3. What real-life experiences helped you draw your conclusion?

_____

 The turtles come onto the beach. Each one digs a hole, puts eggs in the hole, and covers that hole with sand. Then the turtles leave. After several weeks, the baby turtles make their way to the sea.

4. What conclusion can you draw about why the turtles put their eggs in

 the sand? _____

5. What helped you draw this conclusion? _____

_____

6. What real-life experiences helped you draw your conclusion?

 _____

7. How do you think baby turtles got on the beach?

_____

 8. From this paragraph, what can you conclude about where turtles live?

_____

Harcourt

Name _____

▶ Rate each word in the pair as *more positive* or *less positive*. Write your rating on the line next to the word.

1. curious _____   nosy _____

2. weird _____   interesting _____

3. shack _____   cabin _____

4. mushy _____   soft _____

5. sing _____   screech _____

6. suggest _____   demand _____

7. sneaky _____   clever _____

8. smell _____   stink _____

▶ Complete the sentences below.

9. <u>Cool</u> is a little bit different from <u>cold</u>. <u>Warm</u> is a little bit different

from _____ .

10. <u>Frown</u> is a little bit different from <u>cry</u>. <u>Smile</u> is a little bit

different from _____ .

 TRY THIS!   Draw a picture of a sea animal that you like. Then describe it by writing pairs of words that mean about the same thing.

Harcourt

Name _____

▶ **Circle three nouns in each sentence.**

1. Taro and his sister live near Uchiura Bay.

2. Jiro-San called the children on Wednesday.

3. The old man swept the sand with a broom.

4. One night in late July, the turtles came.

5. On a Sunday in September, the eggs hatched.

▶ **List the nouns you circled in the correct column.**

COMMON NOUNS	PROPER NOUNS

SCHOOL-HOME CONNECTION With your child, choose a family member and write several nouns that name that person—for example, *sister, Elinor, swimmer*. Ask that person to add other nouns to the list.

Harcourt

Hidden Surprises **57**

Name _____

▶ **Write the Spelling Word from the box that best completes each sentence.**

chance	such	chew	watch	showed

"It's not every day we get a **(1)** _____ to do this."

"I know, Mom. I like to **(2)** _____ the waves with you."

"Remember when I **(3)** _____ you that whale?"

"Of course! That was **(4)** _____ a spectacular sight!"

"Look! That otter is getting ready to

(5) _____ its food."

▶ **Circle the word that is spelled correctly. Write it on the line.**

6. pushed   puched   _____

7. matck   match   _____

8. shot   chot   _____

Handwriting Tip: Be sure to slant your letters in the same direction. Write these words.

chew

9. shock _____   **10.** crash _____

SCHOOL-HOME CONNECTION With your child, write these words on index cards, and take turns choosing cards and acting them out: *match, watch, showed, pushed, crash,* and *chew.* When a player guesses the word, spell it aloud together. Add other words that have *sh, ch,* and *tch.*

Harcourt

Name _____

▶ **Complete the labels for these photographs by using words from the box.**

creatures	curious	marine	delicate	collapsed	survived

1. These _____ are penguins.

2. _____ iguanas feed in the sea.

3. The sand castle almost _____.

4. He had a battle, but he

_____.

5. Look at this sandpiper's

_____ legs.

6. Is this seagull _____ or just hungry?

▶ **Complete these descriptions with Vocabulary Words.**

7. You could say that a very small flower is _____.

8. A person who does science experiments is _____.

TRY THIS! Draw some pictures of things that would make good photographs. Write captions for your drawings, using the Vocabulary Words.

Harcourt

Name _____

Math

Skill Reminder To draw conclusions, use information from the story and from your own experiences.

▶ Mrs. Warren's class made a graph of their favorite animals. Use the graph to answer the questions.

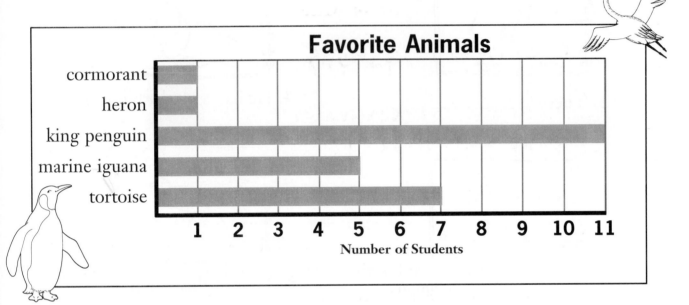

Favorite Animals

Number of Students

1. What conclusions can you draw about the class's favorite animals? _____

_____

2. How many students chose marine iguanas as their favorite? _____

3. How many more students like marine iguanas than herons? _____

4. How many animals got fewer than six votes? _____

5. How many students like king penguins and marine iguanas? _____

6. Why do you think cormorants and herons received the fewest votes?

_____

7. How many students liked the two favorite animals? _____

8. How many students voted altogether? _____

Harcourt

Name _____

Skill Reminder A photo essay is a nonfiction story that has many photographs. Headings may be used to tell about each section of an article.

▶ Read the following article, and then write a heading for each section. Use the headings in the box, or write your own.

Climate in the Galapagos Islands
Animal Life on the Galapagos Islands
Location of the Galapagos Islands
History of the Galapagos Islands

1. _____

Located in the Pacific Ocean, the Galapagos Islands are a group of 13 islands. They are part of the country of Ecuador. Their location is 600 miles off the South American coast.

2. _____

The Galapagos Islands are on the equator, but their climate is cool and mainly dry. The only area that gets a lot of rain is in the high volcanic mountains.

3. _____

In 1535, the Spanish first arrived on the Galapagos Islands. In 1832, people from Ecuador settled the islands.

4. _____

The Galapagos Islands are home to a variety of animal life. Some animals are the giant land tortoise, the marine iguana, and the flightless cormorant, a web-footed water bird with a long neck.

TRY THIS! With a partner, plan a photo essay about an animal you like.

Harcourt

Name _____

▶ Before you begin reading "Wild Shots, They're My Life," complete the first two columns of this chart with what you know about island animals and what you want to know about them. Then, after you finish reading, complete the third column.

K What I Know	W What I Want to Know	L What I Learned

▶ Name one of the animals on the Galapagos Islands you would like to learn more about. Tell why.

_____

_____

_____

Harcourt

Name _____

▶ **Write the word or words from the box that give the meaning of the underlined words.**

jaw	bumpy	ate quickly	area where land meets ocean
sea	groups	pictures	freshwater turtle

1. The penguins were so hungry that they <u>devoured</u> the food.

_____

2. A tortoise has no teeth, but it does have a hard <u>beak</u>.

_____

3. The loggerhead turtle, a <u>terrapin</u>, lives in fresh water.

_____

4. The fish felt rough when I touched its <u>scaly</u> skin.

_____

5. The photographer liked to take close-up <u>shots</u> of animals.

_____

6. Marine iguanas look for food near the water along the

<u>shoreline</u>. _____

7. Although penguins live in large <u>rookeries</u>, they can find their

families easily. _____

8. Penguins live where there is a lot of <u>marine</u> life in the

ocean for them to eat. _____

TRY THIS! Write two sentences using special terms to tell about a hobby or a special interest you have. Explain the special terms.

Hidden Surprises **63**

▶ **Read each sentence. Use context clues to determine the meaning of the underlined word. Then choose the best answer and fill in the oval next to your choice.**

1 Penguins use their <u>flippers</u> and webbed feet to swim. The word *flippers* means

- ⬭ black and white fur.
- ⬭ paddle-like wings.
- ⬭ pointed bills.
- ⬭ rubber swim fins.

2 The photographer had to <u>scurry</u> after the penguins to catch up with them. The word *scurry* means

- ⬭ run slowly.
- ⬭ move away.
- ⬭ run quickly.
- ⬭ move toward.

3 When the young child touched the cactus, its sharp <u>spines</u> stuck in her fingers. The word *spines* means

- ⬭ yellow flowers.
- ⬭ soft needles.
- ⬭ green leaves.
- ⬭ pointed thorns.

4 When marine iguanas are hungry, they <u>graze</u> on seaweed. The word *graze* means

- ⬭ grow.
- ⬭ attach.
- ⬭ feed.
- ⬭ hide.

5 While fighting, one animal <u>punctured</u> the other's skin with its sharp claws. The word *punctured* means

- ⬭ pulled.
- ⬭ cut deeply.
- ⬭ scraped a little.
- ⬭ covered with skin.

6 The <u>hatchlings</u> leave the sea turtle's nest and crawl into the ocean. The word *hatchlings* means

- ⬭ shells.
- ⬭ seagulls.
- ⬭ soft-shelled crabs.
- ⬭ baby sea turtles.

Harcourt

Name _____

▶ **Choose from the box the best reference source to use to find the following information.**

| globe | dictionary | almanac | atlas | encyclopedia |

1. whether the Galapagos Islands are east or west of Hawaii

_____

2. description and picture of a king penguin _____

3. the history of the Galapagos Islands _____

4. the meaning of the word *survived* _____

5. the yearly rainfall in the Galapagos Islands _____

6. pictures and information about elephant seals _____

7. how far the Galapagos Islands are from the United States

_____

8. how to pronounce the word *tortoise* _____

9. where the Pacific Ocean is _____

10. type of weather in Antarctica _____

TRY THIS! Use an encyclopedia to find information about an animal mentioned in "Wild Shots, They're My Life." Write five facts about that animal.

Harcourt

Hidden Surprises **65**

Name _____

▶ **Read the paragraph. Then answer the questions
below.**

Tui De Roy uses a camera for her job. If it is
dark, she uses a <u>flash</u>, which makes light. Sometimes,
Tui De Roy wants to be in the picture herself. Then
she puts the camera on a <u>tripod</u>, a kind of stand. She
sets the <u>self-timer</u> and then walks in front of the
camera. She does not need to press the <u>shutter release</u>. The self-timer tells
the camera when to take the picture. Tui De Roy has a <u>zoom lens</u> for shots
that are far away. A <u>wide-angle lens</u> helps her take a photograph of a wide
area, like a beach. For adding colors, she can put a <u>filter</u> on the lens.

1. Why does Tui De Roy sometimes use a flash?

_____

2. If Tui De Roy wants to be in the picture herself, what does she use?

_____

3. What is a zoom lens used for?

_____

4. What does the self-timer do?

_____

5. What part of a camera do you press to take a picture?

_____

6. What would Tui De Roy use to add color?

_____

7. What is a wide-angle lens used for?

_____

8. How would a diagram help you understand the paragraph?

_____

_____

Harcourt

Name _____

▶ **Circle the nouns. Write *S* above each singular noun.
Write *P* above each plural noun.**

1. The photographer takes pictures of animals.

2. Many strange creatures live on those islands.

3. A cactus makes a tasty treat for that tortoise.

4. The iguanas are fighting over some branches.

5. That seal flaps its flippers on the shore.

▶ **Write the correct plural form of each singular noun.**

6. crab _____

7. monkey _____

8. daisy _____

9. bus _____

10. puppy _____

11. parrot _____

12. canary _____

13. bush _____

14. pouch _____

15. donkey _____

TRY THIS! Look around you. Make a list of ten singular nouns that name things you see. Then write the plural form of each noun.

Harcourt

Name _____

▶ **Write the Spelling Word that best completes each sentence.**

| strange | fence | price | space |

A large crowd was gathered behind a **(1)** _____ at the shore. They were looking at a surfer in a very **(2)** _____ and unusual outfit. He was dressed as a **(3)** _____ explorer instead of as a surfer. I tell you, it was quite a show for a very reasonable **(4)** _____. The cost was nothing!

▶ **Write the Spelling Word from the box that fits each shape.**

| police | office | engine | pencil |

5.

6.

7.

8.

Handwriting Tip: Be sure the letter *g* does not look like a *q*. Write these words.

g

9. stage _____

10. huge _____

SCHOOL-HOME CONNECTION Make up sentences about your child that use words with the /j/ sound and the /s/ sound. (Here are some examples: You are *such a generous person.* You know how to be *gentle* with your baby *sister.* You like to *see* your Aunt *Ginny.*) Have your child make up similar sentences.

Harcourt

Name _____

▶ **Complete each person's sentence with a word from the box.**

| telegraph | drifts | temperature | guided | trail | splinters |

1. The _drifts_ outside is below freezing.

2. Maybe we should send a _temperature_ message to your father.

3. The snow _telegraph_ are getting higher.

4. I'm sure your father can stay on the _trail_.

5. The dogs have _guided_ him home before.

6. Yes, I just hope they don't get any _splinters_ of ice in their paws.

▶ **Complete this sentence with two Vocabulary Words.**

In one tale, a **(7)** _temperature_ of pebbles
(8) _trail_ the children home.

TRY THIS! Think about an outdoor experience you have had. Write three sentences about it, using some of the Vocabulary Words.

Harcourt

Name _____

Skill Reminder Use information from both the story
and what you already know to draw conclusions.

▶ Read the following paragraph. Then write *valid* or
invalid next to each conclusion below.

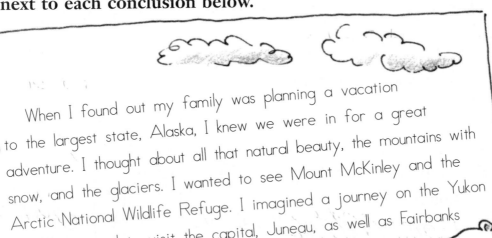

When I found out my family was planning a vacation to the largest state, Alaska, I knew we were in for a great adventure. I thought about all that natural beauty, the mountains with snow, and the glaciers. I wanted to see Mount McKinley and the Arctic National Wildlife Refuge. I imagined a journey on the Yukon River. I wanted to visit the capital, Juneau, as well as Fairbanks and Anchorage. A nearby place I wanted to see was in Canada, the Klondike—the site of the Gold Rush. I couldn't wait to leave for Alaska—"The Land of the Midnight Sun."

1. Alaska is the largest state. _____

2. The author knew his vacation would be boring. _____

3. The Klondike Gold Rush took place in Canada. _____

4. The author is afraid of wild animals. _____

5. The author enjoys skiing on the mountains. _____

6. The author enjoys learning about new places. _____

7. Anchorage is the capital of Alaska. _____

8. The author knows about some places in Alaska. _____

Harcourt

Name _____

Skill Reminder Other words in a sentence can give you clues to the meaning of a new word.

▶ **Read the passage. Use clues in the sentences to figure out what each underlined word means. Write the meanings on the lines.**

The road became slick and **(1)** slippery as the snow turned to ice. City workers, driving big **(2)** tractor trucks, were putting salt on the road in order to **(3)** melt the ice. Once the ice turned back to water, cars would not **(4)** skid and slide off the road. The workers hoped the snowstorm wouldn't turn into a **(5)** blizzard. They knew the **(6)** treacherous winds of a blizzard could be dangerous and mean more snow and ice to handle. Then **(7)** mounds of snow could pile up too high to clear away. But the wind seemed **(8)** calm. The snow was falling slow and straight. That was a good sign.

1. *Slippery* means _____.

2. *Tractor* means _____.

3. *Melt* means _____.

4. *Skid* means _____.

5. *Blizzard* means _____.

6. *Treacherous* means _____.

7. *Mounds* means _____.

8. *Calm* means _____.

TRY THIS! In a science book, find unfamiliar words and their meanings. List and use these words in sentences of your own with clues. Trade with a classmate.

Harcourt

Name _____

▶ As you read "Balto, the Dog Who Saved Nome," fill in the problems that the characters face and the solution to each problem. Remember to think about what the main characters do to solve their problems.

Problem	Solution
	➡
	➡
	➡
	➡
	➡

▶ Why do you think Balto is able to reach Nome?

_____

_____

_____

Harcourt

Name _____

▶ **Read the paragraphs and answer the questions.**

The travelers were in Anchorage and wanted to get to
Nome. However, the snowstorm had caused problems. Roads and train
tracks were blocked with snow. Airplanes couldn't fly. The sea was frozen.

1. What happened to travelers in Anchorage?

_____

2. What would you tell the travelers about travel to Nome?

_____

3. Why would you say this? _____

_____

The two men talked loudly. One man held up his snow-covered hat
and coat, and he pointed to the window. He shook his head. The other
man frowned, put on his boots and coat, and headed for the door.

4. What do you think the two men are talking about?

_____

5. How do you know this?

_____

6. What do you think the other man will do?

_____

7. How do you know this?

_____

8. Do you think the first man will go out in the snow? Why?

_____

Harcourt

Name _____

▶ **Read the definition of each root word. Then finish each sentence below by choosing a word from the box.**

graph = write   *phone* = sound   *therm* = heat

photo = light   *gram* = written   *scope* = see

auto = self   *tele* = far away   *tri* = three

bi = two   *cycle* = circle   *uni* = one

meter = measure

photograph	**telegraph**	**cyclone**	**thermometer**	**bicycle**
telephone	**autograph**	**tricycle**	**telescope**	**unicycle**

1. A _____ can show how hot it is outside.

2. Years ago, written messages were sent to

   faraway places by _____.

3. Please write your name in my _____ book.

4. The _____ rang, but nobody answered it.

5. This _____ helps us see the stars.

6. Katie got a _____, a two-wheeler, for her birthday.

7. My little sister still rides a _____, a three-wheeler.

8. Is it hard to balance on a one-wheeler, a _____?

9. The spinning _____ hit as we got into the cellar.

10. The light of the sunset was perfect for this _____.

TRY THIS! Write a short note to a friend. Use at least three words that are formed from the root words above.

Harcourt

Name _____

▶ **Underline the irregular noun in each sentence.
Write whether each noun you underline is
singular or *plural*.**

1. Have you ever seen a goose?

   _____

2. Many mice live up here.

   _____

3. Their teeth are very sharp.

   _____

4. That moose is looking at me.

   _____

5. The men all walk away.

   _____

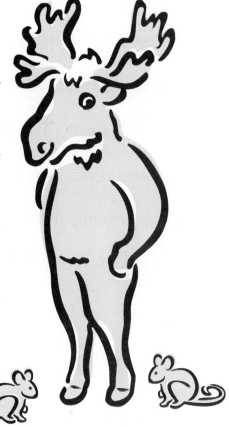

▶ **Write the correct plural form of each singular noun. Use a
dictionary if necessary.**

6. woman _____   11. goose _____

7. deer _____   12. child _____

8. sheep _____   13. foot _____

9. trout _____   14. tooth _____

10. man _____   15. mouse _____

 TRY THIS! Pick one singular noun and one plural noun from your list above.
Use both words in a single sentence.

Harcourt

Name _____

▶ **Write Spelling Words to finish the rhymes.**

choice	spoil	employ	royal	voice	annoy

In a strong, clear **(1)** _____,

She made her **(2)** _____.

They made a dinner quite **(3)** _____,

So the food would not **(4)** _____.

I know this might **(5)** _____ you,

But I no longer can **(6)** _____ you.

▶ **Write the Spelling Word from the box that goes with each clue.**

cowboy	joint	moist	noise

7. slightly wet _____

9. together _____

8. cattle driver _____

10. sound _____

Handwriting Tip: Make sure an *i* does not look like an *e*.
Write these words.

11. voice _____

12. noise _____

SCHOOL-HOME CONNECTION Make up sentences with your child, using words that have the /oi/ sound. Start with the Spelling Words, and then add words such as *coin*, *enjoy*, and *oyster*.

Harcourt

Name _____

▶ **Write the word from the box that answers
each riddle.**

allergic	erupting	brunch	omelet
	escape	lava	peaceful

1. I come out of active volcanoes.

   What am I? _____

2. I am another word for *run away*.

   What am I? _____

3. I'm a food made from eggs.

   What am I? _____

4. I am a meal served between breakfast and lunch time.

   What am I? _____

5. I am a word that tells what a volcano is doing when it is exploding.

   What am I? _____

6. I am the opposite of *noisy*. What am I? _____

7. Life in the village was quiet and _____.
   Then the volcano erupted.

8. I sneeze when I go outside because I am

   _____ to grass.

SCHOOL-HOME CONNECTION With your child, make a
"Hidden Words" puzzle, using Vocabulary Words. Give the
puzzle to a family member to solve.

Hidden Surprises **77**

Harcourt

Skill Reminder **Clues from other words and phrases in a sentence can help you understand a word that is not familiar.**

▶ Circle words in each sentence that help give the meaning of the underlined words. On the line, write the word's meaning.

1. Little Grunt's mom used eggs and greens to make an <u>omelet</u>.

   Omelet means _____.

2. The Grunt family has <u>brunch</u> instead of breakfast and lunch.

   Brunch means _____.

3. The dinosaur changed the family's quiet and <u>peaceful</u> life.

   Peaceful means _____.

4. The melted rock, or <u>lava</u>, flowing from the volcano would be hot.

   Lava means _____.

5. As the volcano began <u>erupting</u>, lava shot out from the earth.

   Erupting means _____.

6. Big rocks, huge stones, and <u>boulders</u> fell near the cave.

   Boulders means _____.

7. The chief would <u>resign</u>, and there would not be anyone to lead.

   Resign means _____.

8. The Grunt family was able to get away or <u>escape</u> being hurt by the volcano.

   Escape means _____.

Harcourt

Name _____

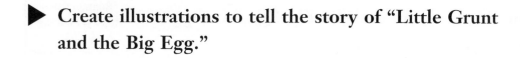
▶ **Create illustrations to tell the story of "Little Grunt and the Big Egg."**

1. Draw a picture showing where the story takes place.

2. Draw the main characters in that setting.

3. Draw pictures to show the main events that happen.

4. Draw a picture to show the problem and how it is solved.

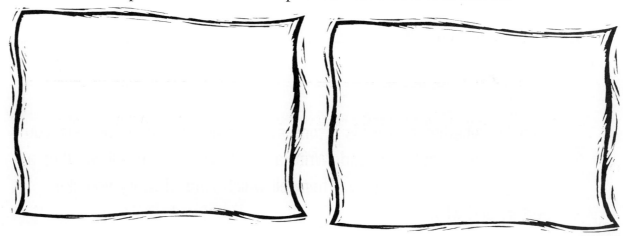

Harcourt

Name _____

▶ As you read "Little Grunt and the Big Egg," complete
the following chart.

	Reality	Fantasy
	Things That Can Really Happen	Things That Cannot Really Happen
Setting		
Characters		
Events		

▶ Answer the following questions.

1. Is this story a fantasy or a realistic story? _____

2. How do you know? _____

_____

Knowing whether a story is a fantasy or realistic fiction can help you
decide which books to read. Write about how you can tell whether a
story is realistic or fantasy. Then tell which kind of story you like
better, and why.

Harcourt

Name _____

▶ **Read these sentences about "Little Grunt and the Big Egg." Put an _R_ after sentences telling about something that could happen in real life. Put an _F_ after sentences telling about something that could only happen in a fantasy story.**

1. Little Grunt knows eggs break easily. _____

2. Little Grunt has a dinosaur for a pet. _____

3. Dinosaurs make nice pets. _____

4. Little Grunt misses his pet. _____

5. When a volcano erupts, steam, rocks, and black smoke come out of

the ground. _____

6. The lava pours out of the volcano and heads for a cave. _____

7. A dinosaur rescues cave people. _____

8. A dinosaur and cave people live happily ever after. _____

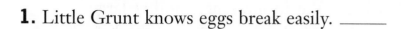

▶ **Answer these questions about "Little Grunt and the Big Egg."**

9. What is the most realistic part of this story?

_____

10. What is the most fantastic part of this story?

_____

_____

Harcourt

SCHOOL-HOME CONNECTION With your child, look
through the comics in a newspaper for stories of things
that could really happen and things that are fantasies.

Name _____

▶ **Read the paragraph. Look for clues to the meaning of each underlined word. Write the meanings of the underlined words on the lines below.**

Dinosaurs were prehistoric reptiles. They lived before history was written down. The tyrannosaur, a huge dinosaur, was a meat eater. On the other hand, the brontosaur, another large dinosaur, was herbivorous. It ate only plants. Scientists study dinosaurs from their bones. Minerals in the ground turned the bones to stone, just like petrified wood.

1. A *dinosaur* was .

2. *Prehistoric* means _____

_____.

3. A *tyrannosaur* was _____.

4. A *brontosaur* was .

5. *Herbivorous* means _____.

6. *Scientists* _____.

7. *Minerals* are .

8. *Petrified* means .

 TRY THIS! Look in a history book or a social studies book for at least four new words. Use clues to figure out the meanings. Then use each word in a sentence of your own.

Harcourt

Name _____

▶ **Circle the possessive noun in each sentence.**

1. That dinosaur's appetite is huge.

2. It ate all of Mama's pancakes.

3. Then it ate the family's lunch and dinner.

4. The tribe's chief has had enough.

5. He wants the baby's pet to leave.

▶ **Rewrite each phrase, using singular possessive nouns.**

6. the home that belongs to the caveman

_____

7. the egg of the creature _____

8. the tail of the lizard _____

9. the pet that belongs to the boy _____

10. the members of the tribe _____

11. the leg of the woman _____

12. the pots owned by Mama _____

TRY THIS! Think of a pet a friend or relative owns. Write three sentences about that pet. Use a different singular possessive noun in each sentence.

Harcourt

Name _____

▶ Write the Spelling Word that goes with each clue.

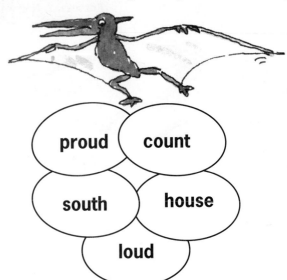

proud   count   south   house   loud

1. not humble   _____

2. not quiet   _____

3. opposite of north _____

4. home   _____

5. one, two, three _____

▶ Write the Spelling Word that fits each shape.

however

around

shouted

6.

7.

8.

Handwriting Tip: Make sure a *w* does not look like a *v*. Write these words.

_____

w

9. crown _____   **10.** crowded _____

SCHOOL-HOME CONNECTION With your child, make up sentences with words that have the /ow/ sound you hear in *wow*. Use the sentences to tell a story.

Harcourt

Name _____

▶ **On the lines below, write the word from a kite that matches each definition.**

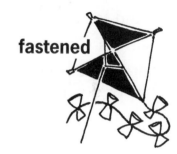

cartwheel   lonely   mustache   beyond   seriously   fastened

1. a sideways handspring or a tumbling move _____

2. attached or tied together _____

3. in a thoughtful way _____

4. the hair on a man's upper lip _____

5. feeling alone and wishing for company _____

6. farther away than _____

▶ **Complete each sentence with a Vocabulary Word.**

7. The park is far away, and the river is _____ it.

8. A clown talks in a silly way, but a business person speaks

_____ .

SCHOOL-HOME CONNECTION With your child, write one
Vocabulary Word and draw pictures around the word so the
page looks like a collage.

Name _____

Skill Reminder   Use reference sources to find
information about a topic or to check information.

▶ **Read the paragraphs. Then write the name of the
best reference source to use to find information about
the underlined topics.**

Kites are made of paper, plastic, or cloth and a lightweight frame.
They are flown in the wind by holding a cord wrapped around a stick.
Most kites are in diamond, hexagon, or tetrahedron shapes. The best
wind for flying kites is between 13 and 32 kilometers per hour. In places
such as China and Japan, kite festivals are held. In fact, in these countries,
kites have been flown for thousands of years.

People have used kites for fun and also for research. Benjamin Franklin
flew a kite during a thunderstorm to learn about lightning.

1. pictures of kites _____

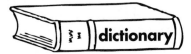
dictionary

2. the meaning of the word *lightweight* _____

3. the pronunciation of the word *tetrahedron* _____

4. how to change kilometers to miles _____

5. the location of China _____

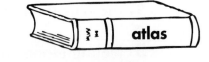
atlas

6. what body of water Japan is near _____

7. names of kite festivals _____

8. who Benjamin Franklin was _____

globe

encyclopedia   almanac

**TRY
THIS!**
Use an encyclopedia to find information about the first kites. Write a
paragraph telling what you learned.

Harcourt

86 Hidden Surprises

Name _____

▶ As you read "The Stories Julian Tells," complete the sequence diagram below. Remember to write the events in the same order in which they happen in the story.

Sequence Diagram

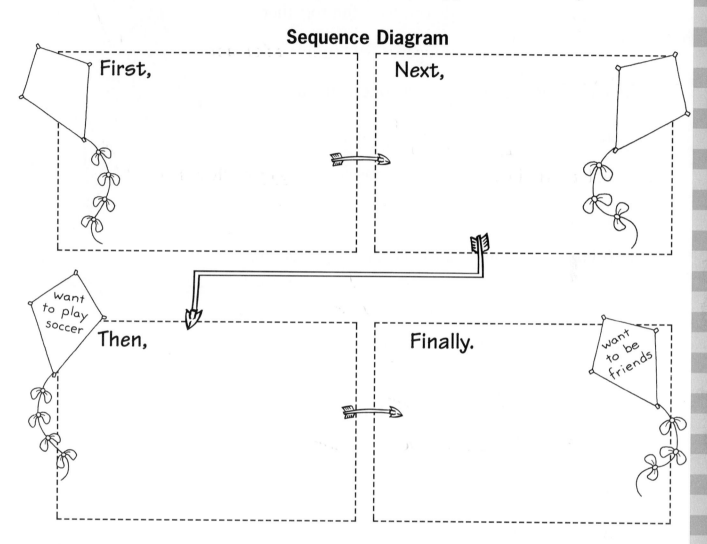

First,

Next,

Then,

want to play soccer

Finally.

want to be friends

▶ Describe the first thing that happens that makes Julian sure he will like Gloria.

_____

_____

_____

 TRY THIS! Write about a favorite thing you like to do with someone special, such as a friend or a relative.

Harcourt

Name _____

▶ **Choose the word that is close to the meaning of the underlined word in each sentence. Write it on the line.**

1. People who are <u>friends</u> can have fun together.

   a. pals   **b.** strangers   _____

2. A <u>walk</u> can be fun with someone you like.

   a. ride   **b.** stroll   _____

3. If you aren't <u>sure</u> about your answers, check them again.

   a. certain   **b.** doubtful   _____

4. If you are <u>unhappy</u>, a friend can cheer you up.

   a. glad   **b.** sad   _____

▶ **Choose the word that means the opposite of the underlined word in each sentence. Write it on the line.**

5. Friends always want the <u>best</u> for you.

   a. greatest   **b.** worst   _____

6. A friend will say a <u>kind</u> word if you make a mistake.

   a. thoughtful   **b.** cruel   _____

7. If you <u>lose</u> something, a friend will help look for it.

   a. find   **b.** misplace   _____

8. You can <u>always</u> depend on a friend.

   a. never   **b.** forever   _____

 TRY THIS! Write a synonym and an antonym for each of these words: *answer, same, start, right, light.*

Harcourt

Name _____

▶ **Choose the best answer. Fill in the oval next to your choice.**

1 Which word is a synonym for *group*?

  ⬭ individual

  ⬭ one

  ⬭ set

  ⬭ each

2 Which word is an antonym for *curly*?

  ⬭ wavy

  ⬭ pretty

  ⬭ bouncy

  ⬭ straight

3 Which pair of words are synonyms?

  ⬭ tried, attempted

  ⬭ tried, failed

  ⬭ failed, succeeded

  ⬭ won, lost

4 Which pair of words are antonyms?

  ⬭ small, tiny

  ⬭ small, large

  ⬭ delicate, fragile

  ⬭ delicate, dainty

5 Which pair of words are synonyms?

  ⬭ old, young

  ⬭ right, wrong

  ⬭ leave, arrive

  ⬭ while, during

6 Which pair of words are antonyms?

  ⬭ go, leave

  ⬭ come, go

  ⬭ sea, ocean

  ⬭ idea, thought

Name _____

► Complete the similes below by writing a word or
words on each line. You can use the words on the
kites or your own words.

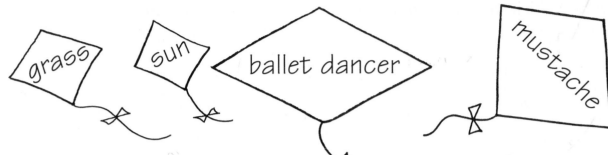

1. The kites are made of paper

   as green as _____.
2. Gloria's smile is as bright as the

   _____.

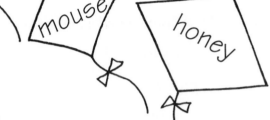

3. The kite's tail moved back and forth like a

   _____.
4. The fruit juice is as sweet

   as _____.

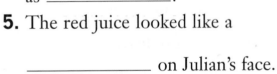

5. The red juice looked like a

   _____ on Julian's face.

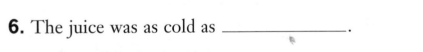

6. The juice was as cold as _____.

7. The kite fluttered to the ground like a _____.

8. Gloria and Julian ran home as fast as the _____.

9. Gloria did cartwheels as gracefully as a _____.

10. Julian was as quiet as a _____.

TRY THIS! Make labels for five things around your classroom. Use a simile in
each label.

Name _Samuel Marsh_

▶ **Write the plural possessive noun in each sentence.**

1. The boys' parents work hard. _boys'_

2. The neighbors' yards are neat. _neighbors'_

3. Where are the racers' bicycles? _racers'_

4. The bikes' tires are flat. _bikes'_

5. Julian pretends to drive his parents' car. _pretends'_

▶ **Rewrite each phrase, using a plural possessive noun.**

6. the kites of the girls

the girls kites

7. the games of the friends

the friends games

8. the nests of the birds

birds nests

9. the jobs of the adults

The adults jobs

10. the bones of the puppies

The puppies bones

TRY THIS! Write three plural nouns that end with _s_. Then write the plural possessive form of each noun you wrote.

Harcourt

Name _Samuel Marsh_

▶ **Write the word that best completes each phrase.**

man's   men's

1. this group of
man's hats

man's   men's

3. the _man's_ hat

uncles   uncle's

2. the _uncles_ clock

brothers   brother's

4. the _brothers_
and the cat

▶ **Write the word that best completes the sentence.**

5. I have three _uncles_. **(uncles   uncle's)**

6. This is my _sisters_ room. **(sisters   sister's)**

7. My _brothers_ hair is red. **(brothers   brother's)**

8. The twin _sisters_ dresses are pretty. **(sister's   sisters')**

Handwriting Tip: When you write an _s_, bring the first upstroke
to a point. If it is rounded, it might look like an _o_. Write these words.

9. sisters _sisters_   10. child's _childs_

Harcourt

SCHOOL-HOME CONNECTION With your child, write labels for various
items in the home to indicate possession. Here are a few examples:
Mom's shoes, the dog's dish, the family's TV, the kids' playroom.

Name _____

▶ **Complete each sentence with a word from one of the bees.**

1. We moved the volleyball net out of

the _____ so we could use the
space for a talent show.

2. The audience seems to be

_____ the show.

3. Paul is going to play a drum solo.

I can't wait to see him _____!

4. Marco plans to _____ a poem.

5. Angela and Monica _____
to do a dance.

6. Keisha wants to tell about the _____
of stars in the sky.

recite

billions

enjoying

gym

▶ **Write the Vocabulary Word that means
the opposite.**

7. disliking   _____

8. a few   _____

prefer

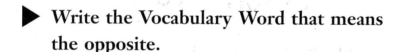

perform

 TRY THIS! Imagine that your school is having a talent show, and you're in it. What
do you plan to do? Write a paragraph about your act. Use as many of
the Vocabulary Words as you can.

Harcourt

Name _____

▶ As you begin reading "The Talent Show," fill in the first three boxes of the Prediction Diagram below. After you finish reading, complete the last box.

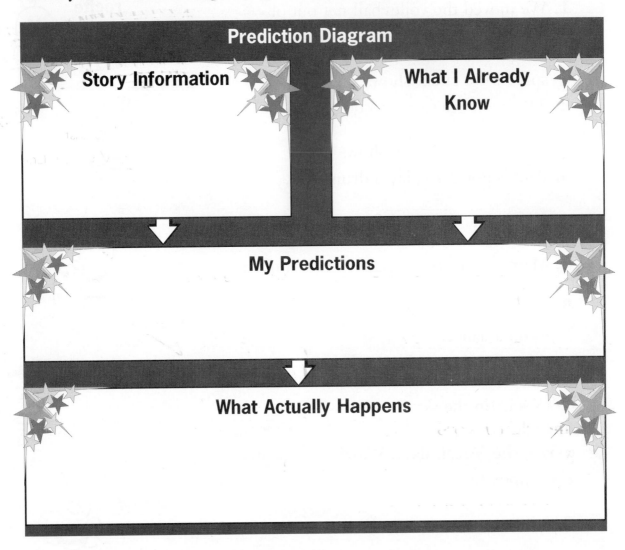

Prediction Diagram

Story Information

What I Already Know

My Predictions

What Actually Happens

▶ Why is Beany unhappy working with Carol Ann?

_____

_____

_____

TRY THIS! Write about a talent show you have been in or have seen. Describe the acts you liked the best.

Harcourt

Skill Reminder Synonyms are words that mean the same thing. Antonyms are words that mean the opposite.

▶ In the newspaper story, find and write the synonym for each underlined word.

1. show

_____

2. spectacular

_____

3. students

_____

4. truly

_____

The talent show at school last night was just spectacular. Many students gave a wonderful performance. Some pupils from Mrs. Eaton's third-grade class did magic tricks that were truly amazing. This reporter really could not tell how the tricks were done.

▶ In each sentence, find and write the antonym for each underlined word.

5. The girl who sang seemed very underline{confident} and not a bit nervous.

_____

6. Carol Ann thought her joke was the best, but it was really the worst.

_____

7. There was not enough room for everyone in the audience to sit, so

some people had to stand. _____

8. After the noise of the ten-minute applause, the silence was a relief.

_____

TRY THIS! In a book, find five words for which you can write synonyms and five words for which you can write antonyms. Start a list of synonyms and antonyms.

Harcourt

Name _____

▶ Suppose Beany got a new science book. Write what part of the book she would look in to find the information listed below. Choose from the book parts in the box.

| table of contents | glossary | copyright page | cover | index |

1. how many chapters are in the book

_____

2. when the book was published

_____

3. the title of the book

_____

4. where to find information about bees

_____

5. what the word *billions* means

_____

▶ Write what you know about guide words. Answer these questions.

6. Where are guide words in a dictionary or an encyclopedia located?

_____

7. What do guide words tell you? _____

_____

8. After finding the guide words, what is the next step in locating a word?

_____

Harcourt

▶ On the line, write the word from the box that comes between each pair of guide words. Use alphabetical order.

| bus | dark | dairy | bee |

1. bean _____ boat

2. boss _____ button

3. dance _____ day

4. dad _____ damp

▶ Suppose Beany uses a nonfiction book about bees. Fill in the chart. Write the part of the book she would look in to find the following information.

Information Beany Needs	Where to Look
title of book	**5.**
kinds of bees	**6.**
what chapter tells where bees live	**7.**
the word *solitary*	**8.**

Name _____

▶ **On the lines below, write the shortened forms of the underlined words.**

1. Let's design an advertisement for the talent show.

4. I'll need a telephone to use in my act.

5. I'll need a white laboratory coat.

2. Will the show be in the gymnasium?

6. I'm going to pretend I'm a veterinarian.

3. Marie, make sure the microphone is working.

7. I hope I don't come down with influenza before the show.

1. _____   5. _____

2. _____   6. _____

3. _____   7. _____

4. _____

▶ **On the lines below, write three words used when talking about a computer.**

8. _____   10. _____

9. _____

TRY THIS! Nicknames are another form of clipped words. Write a list of names and their nicknames, based on the names of people you know.

Harcourt

Name _____

► **Rewrite these abbreviations correctly.**

1. dr Kerry _____

2. mr Sands _____

3. apr 17 _____

4. wed _____

5. Grand Ave _____

6. jan 15 _____

7. tues _____

8. High st _____

9. ms ruhl _____

10. mrs ford _____

► **Rewrite each phrase, using abbreviations correctly.**

11. December 20 _____

12. Lambert Road _____

13. August 14 _____

14. Thursday, May 9 _____

15. February 12 _____

16. Mister Yung _____

17. Central Avenue _____

18. Doctor Soto _____

19. Sunday, November 3 _____

20. Long Lake Street _____

SCHOOL-HOME CONNECTION With your child, make a list of the birthdays in your family. Abbreviate the name of the month for each birthday. Post the list where everyone at home can see it.

Hidden Surprises

Name _____

▶ **Write the Spelling Words that best complete the story.**

| taught | song | because | pause | crawl |

We had a family talent show. My baby brother had just

learned to **(1)** _____, so he did that. My sister sang a

(2) _____. Dad had **(3)** _____ me

the drums, but I had to **(4)** _____ in the middle

of my act. My mom clapped loudly **(5)** _____,
she said, everyone was great.

▶ **Write the Spelling Word from the box that goes with each clue.**

| law | dawn | lost |

6. sunrise _____

7. rhymes with *cost* _____

8. rule _____

Handwriting Tip: Make sure an *o* does not look like an *a*.
Write these words.

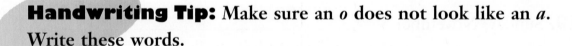

9. long _____   **10.** soft _____

SCHOOL-HOME CONNECTION Walk around your neighborhood
with your child. Look for things whose names have the sound you
hear in *walk*, such as *lawns*, *awnings*, *paws*, and *claws*.

Harcourt

Name _____

► Complete each sentence with a word or words from the box.

firm	confident	comfortable	approach
equipment	program	appointment	

1. Training begins today. The

_____ director said to

be here at noon.

2. I had to change the time of my dentist

_____ so we could be here.

3. Trixie has a leash, and I think that

is all the _____ we need.

4. I am very _____ that my

dog will learn a lot.

5. I want my dog to be _____

with people.

6. I want my dog to learn to

_____ people only

when called, and to listen when

I speak in a _____ voice.

► **Answer these questions using Vocabulary Words.**

7. Which word can describe a show on television?

_____

8. Which word can mean "not too hot or cold"? _____

SCHOOL-HOME CONNECTION With your child, talk about a
class or an activity you know about. As you talk, try to use at
least three of the Vocabulary Words.

Harcourt

Name _____

Skill Reminder Use different reference sources in the library to locate information.

▶ Read each definition. Write the name of the reference source from the box that best fits each definition.

| atlas | dictionary | phone book | almanac |
| card catalog or computer database | encyclopedia | newspaper | thesaurus |

1. has lists of all books found in the library by title, subject, and author

   _____

2. has yearly information and facts about many

   topics such as sports, population, climate _____

3. has synonyms for words _____

4. has telephone numbers and advertisements _____

5. has word meanings and pronunciations _____

6. has information on important people, places, and events,

   arranged in alphabetical order _____

7. has different kinds of maps _____

8. has information on today's weather, movies,

   local and world news _____

TRY THIS! Look through a dictionary. Find meanings for these words: *volunteer, canine,* and *harness*. Write each word in a sentence.

Harcourt

Name _____

Skill Reminder **Many words have multiple meanings.**
Use the context of the sentence to determine the
meaning that is wanted.

▶ Read the diary entry. For each underlined word, write on the line
the meaning that is used in the diary entry. Choose from the words
in parentheses ( ).

Dear Diary,
    Today I had company—a
visiting dog! The dog let me
groom him. I used a brush and
took tangles out of his coat.
Then the dog sat on my lap.

A woman said the dog had
taken a course to learn to be
polite and that the dog had
learned fast. I might meet the
dog's owners next week.

1. company (a business, a visitor or visitors)

_____

2. groom (to take care of, a man getting married)

_____

3. coat (a jacket, an animal's skin or fur)

_____

4. lap (a part of the body, to drink as an animal does)

_____

5. course (a field for sports, a series of lessons)

_____

6. fast (to go without food, quickly) _____

7. might (may, great strength) _____

8. meet (to be introduced to, a race) _____

Hidden Surprises **103**

Name _____

Skill Reminder Synonyms are words that are close in meaning. Antonyms are words that have opposite meanings.

▶ In the weather report, find and write the synonym for each underlined word.

Today was <u>rainy</u>, and tomorrow will be rainy, <u>too</u>. Thursday is also likely to be a bit drizzly. On Thursday afternoon, however, the sun will come out. This will <u>allow</u> you to take your <u>dogs</u> to the park. Just let those pooches run <u>fast</u> and enjoy themselves, because the rain may quickly return.

1. rainy _____

2. too _____

3. allow _____

4. dogs _____

5. fast _____

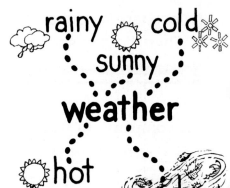

rainy   cold   sunny   weather   hot   windy

▶ In each sentence, find and write the antonym for the underlined word.

6. This <u>gentle</u> dog is never rough with anyone. _____

7. We <u>began</u> at 5:00 P.M. and stopped at 6:00 P.M. _____

8. The dog wanted to <u>stay</u>, but we had to go. _____

9. I can throw the ball <u>high</u> or low. _____

10. This dog was a <u>wild</u> puppy, but it is now tame. _____

TRY THIS! Write five sentences about a pet. Then choose five words in the sentences and write synonyms and antonyms for each.

Harcourt

Name _____

▶ As you read "Rosie, a Visiting Dog's Story," complete
the sequence chart below. Remember to enter the
information in the order in which it appears in the book.

Kinds of Training	What Rosie Learned

▶ Write a few sentences describing the effect Rosie had on some of the
people she visited.

_____

_____

_____

Harcourt

Name _____

▶ **Read the paragraphs below, and think about the main idea. Then answer the questions.**

Now that Rosie is a visiting dog, she is very busy. She has a lot of places to visit, such as hospitals, retirement homes, and children's homes. Rosie visits people almost every day.

Rosie is a great visiting dog. She loves being around all kinds of people. She especially likes people who rub her fur and talk to her. She loves snuggling close and making people feel happy. Both older people and younger people love to see Rosie.

1. What is the main idea of the first paragraph?

_____

_____

2. Is this idea stated, or told, in the paragraph? If so, where?

_____

3. What is the main idea of the second paragraph?

_____

_____

4. What information in the rest of the paragraph helps you know what

the main idea is? _____

_____

TRY THIS! Work with a partner. Create a poster that shows in pictures and in words what a main idea is.

Harcourt

Name _____

▶ **Read the paragraph. Then answer the questions. Fill in the oval next to your choice.**

There are many stories, television shows, and movies that have a dog as the main character. One reason dogs are so popular is that they are easy to train. Another reason is that audiences love to imagine dogs rescuing people or other animals who are in danger. Finally, many dogs are cuddly, playful, and cute.

1 What is the main idea of this paragraph?

⬭ Dogs are cute.

⬭ A dog is the main character of many stories, television shows, and movies.

⬭ Dogs are easy to train.

⬭ Dogs rescue people and other animals who are in danger.

2 In what part of the paragraph is the main idea stated?

⬭ the first sentence

⬭ the second sentence

⬭ the third sentence

⬭ the fourth sentence

3 Which sentence is another way of saying the main idea of the paragraph?

⬭ Dogs are popular characters because they are cute and cuddly.

⬭ Dogs make great main characters of books and movies.

⬭ Television shows and movies with dogs are watched by a lot of people.

⬭ Television shows, movies, and books often have a dog as the main character.

4 The main idea of a paragraph is always

⬭ full of details.

⬭ the first sentence.

⬭ the most important point.

⬭ the last sentence.

Harcourt

Name _____

▶ **Make a new word by adding a word from the box to each word below. Then write the new word.**

| son | side | book | bone | up |
| print | day | chair | noon | room |

1. some + _____ = _____

2. along + _____ = _____

3. wheel + _____ = _____

4. class + _____ = _____

5. check + _____ = _____

6. after + _____ = _____

7. grand + _____ = _____

8. text + _____ = _____

9. foot + _____ = _____

10. back + _____ = _____

TRY THIS! Write parts of compound words on separate index cards. Mix the cards, and lay them face down on a desk or table. Pick two cards at a time. If both cards make one word, you've made a match!

Harcourt

Name _____

▶ **Write the pronoun in each sentence. Put _S_ beside it if it is a singular pronoun, and _P_ if it is a plural pronoun.**

1. Robin trained her in the park. _____

2. They work together every day. _____

3. I would like to have a visiting dog. _____

4. Maybe we should learn to train a dog. _____

5. The dogs were fun and the kids loved them. _____

▶ **Rewrite each sentence. Use a singular or plural pronoun to replace the underlined word or words.**

6. That <u>girl</u> uses a wheelchair.

_____

7. <u>My friend Richard</u> is in the hospital.

_____

8. Janis met <u>Anita</u> at a class for training dogs.

_____

9. <u>Those dogs</u> seem very smart.

_____

10. Did that dog like <u>the leash</u>?

_____

 TRY THIS! Write three sentences about someone you know. Use pronouns to avoid repeating nouns. Have a classmate read your sentences and tell you whether your use of pronouns is clear.

Name _____

▶ Write the Spelling Word from the box that matches each picture.

boots	hood	balloon	cooking

1. _hood_

3. _cooking_

2. _boots_

4. _balloon_

▶ Unscramble the letters, and write the correct Spelling Word from the words in the box.

grouped	shook	school	looked	choose	loose

koodel   5. _looked_   dogrupe   8. _grouped_

kosoh   6. _shook_   locsoh   9. _school_

sohoce   7. _choose_   elsoo   10. _loose_

Handwriting Tip: Space your letters properly. Write these words.

cool

11. loose _lose_

12. school _school_

SCHOOL-HOME CONNECTION With your child, find things whose names have the vowel sounds you hear in *book* and in *boot*. For example, you might find *wool, cookbook, balloon,* and *shampoo.*

Harcourt

Name _____

▶ **Complete each sentence with a word from the box.**

| ballhawk | vanish | fault | concentrate | outfielder | depend |

1. That ball you hit seemed to _____ into the air!

2. That's right! We really _____ on your hitting!

3. It was my _____ the other team got that third run.

4. That's not true! No _____ could have caught that ball.

5. I really tried to _____ on my fielding today.

6. Well, you're a real _____. Not too much gets by you!

▶ **Solve these equations using Vocabulary Words.**

7. a toy + a bird = _____

8. not in + meadow + *er* = _____

 TRY THIS! Make up your own titles for three books about sports. Use one Vocabulary Word in each title. Then draw a book cover for one of your books.

Harcourt

Name _____

Skill Reminder   The main idea is the one idea most of the sentences in a paragraph tell about.

▶ **Read each paragraph. Then answer the questions.**

Playing baseball is a good way to exercise. When hitting the ball, you use the muscles in your arms. Then you run the bases. The other team sometimes has to run after the ball in order to catch it.

1. Which sentence tells the main idea?

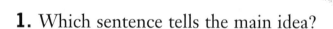

2. Why is this the main idea?

Birds such as the robin and blue jay build their nests in the city. The gray jay and the brown creeper live in forests. Other types of birds live in grasslands. The roadrunner is a desert bird. Many owls also live in the desert. Ducks live near water.

3. What is the main idea? Tell in your own words.

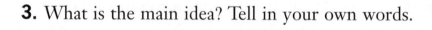

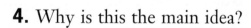

4. Why is this the main idea?

Harcourt

Name _____

Skill Reminder You can find information in many different kinds of reference sources.

▶ Write the source you would use to answer each question below.

1. Which baseball player hit the most home runs in 1998?

_____

2. What does the word *lambasted*

mean? _____

3. What did the first baseman of the Little League team say to a

reporter? _____

_____

4. When and where was the first baseball game played?

_____

5. What was the score of a baseball game played yesterday?

_____

6. What player had the best batting average during the 1998–1999 season?

_____

▶ Suppose you use a dictionary and an encyclopedia to locate information about tennis. Write the kind of information you would probably find in each reference source.

7. Dictionary entry: _____

_____

8. Encyclopedia entry: _____

_____

SCHOOL-HOME CONNECTION With your child, find a newspaper or magazine article about an athlete. Read the article together, and talk about information you find in the article.

Hidden Surprises **113**

Name _____

▶ Complete the story map as you read "Centerfield
Ballhawk." List only the important events.

Story Map

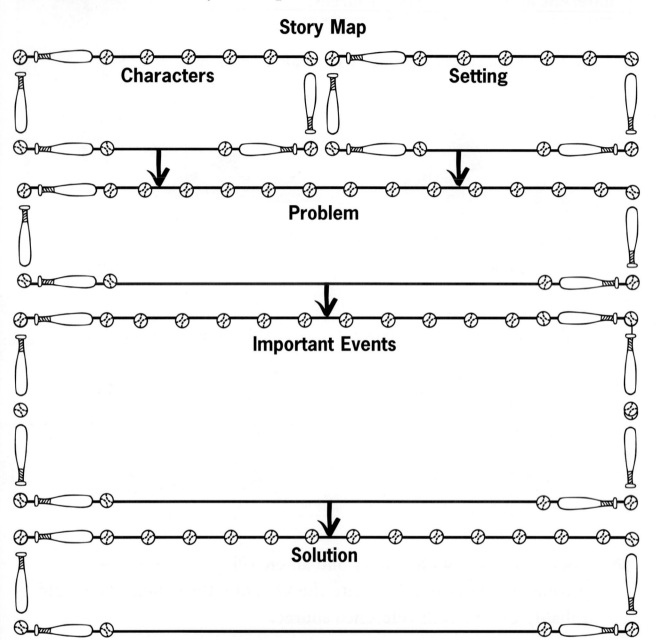

Characters   **Setting**

Problem

Important Events

Solution

▶ What was more important to José, baseball or
his family? Explain how you know.

_____

_____

_____

Name _____

▶ **The underlined word in each sentence is a homograph. Choose and then write the correct meaning of each underlined word.**

1. The ball went so high that it seemed to take a <u>minute</u> before landing.

    a. 60 seconds   **b.** very small   _____

2. The <u>bat</u> was too heavy for the hitter.

    a. a flying animal   **b.** a wooden stick   _____

3. He hit the ball too <u>close</u> to the neighbor's window.

    a. shut   **b.** near   _____

4. He <u>stands</u> up when his team wins.

    a. to be on one's feet   **b.** booths   _____

5. The team gave him a baseball for a <u>present</u>.

    a. at this time   **b.** a gift   _____

▶ **Write the pair of homophones in each sentence.**

6. He had to wait his turn to check his weight.    _____

7. From right here, I can hear the music.   _____

8. I always write with my right hand.   _____

9. There is no way to know what pitch is next.   _____

10. The last two batters were able to get hits.   _____

Harcourt

SCHOOL-HOME CONNECTION With your child, make a list of homophones and homographs. Choose two pairs of each type, and write silly sentences for the words. Then read them to other family members.

Name _____

▶ **Replace the underlined verb or phrase in each sentence with a more vivid verb. Choose from the verbs in the bat, or use your own verbs. Write the new sentence**

blasted

skittered

leaped

sailed

trotted

pounded

screamed

raced

zoomed

moaned

1. Barry <u>hit</u> the ball hard.

_____

2. The ball <u>bounced</u> along the ground.

_____

3. The next ball <u>went</u> over the fence.

_____

4. The fans <u>jumped</u> to their feet.

_____

5. Barry <u>ran</u> slowly around the bases.

_____

6. The fans <u>said</u>, "Here comes Joanne!"

_____

7. Joanne <u>hit</u> the ball firmly.

_____

8. Then she <u>ran</u> to first base.

_____

9. The ball <u>went</u> out to center field.

_____

10. The team <u>sounded disappointed</u>.

_____

Harcourt

Name _____

▶ **Write the subject pronoun in each sentence.**

1. She hit a home run in that game. _____

2. He made an amazing catch. _____

3. I was proud of the two children. _____

4. They had practiced hard. _____

5. It was the first game the team had won. _____

▶ **Rewrite each sentence. Use a subject pronoun to replace each underlined phrase.**

6. José's father was a ballplayer.

   _____

7. Many pitchers went up against him.

   _____

8. His bat looks old and battered.

   _____

9. You and I play for fun.

   _____

10. The mitts and balls are in my bag.

   _____

TRY THIS! Write a sentence with a compound subject. Then rewrite the sentence, using a subject pronoun to replace the subject.

Hidden Surprises **117**

Name _____

▶ **Write the Spelling Words from the box that best complete the sentences.**

part	barn	started	star

We got **(1)** _____ a little late. The train is going

through a beautiful **(2)** _____ of the country right now.

I saw a red **(3)** _____ on a farm. Someone had painted a

(4) _____ and a cloud on it.

▶ **Use the Spelling Words in the box and the clues below to complete the puzzle.**

smart	shark	sharp	mark

Down

5. to label

6. pointed

Across

7. dangerous fish

8. intelligent

Handwriting Tip: Be sure your letters sit evenly on the bottom line. Write these words.

star

9. party _____   **10.** card _____

SCHOOL-HOME CONNECTION With your child, make up phrases with rhyming words that have the /är/ sound you hear in *yard*. Here are some examples: *a lark in the park, a car with a star.*

Harcourt

▶ **Finish this diary entry. Use words from the box to complete the sentences.**

glanced	comfort	longed	contagious
prescription	attention	unexpected	

Dear Diary,

Monday

Today I **(1)** _____ at myself in the

mirror and saw an **(2)** _____ sight. I had

red spots on my face! Measles is a **(3)** _____

sickness, so now I have to stay home. Myra says I am just

trying to get **(4)** _____, but I really feel bad.

Tuesday

I feel a little bit better today. It is a **(5)** _____

to think about swimming in the cool lake last summer.

When we got home again, I **(6)** _____

to go back! Well, it is time for me to go take more of my

(7) _____ medicine.

▶ **Write sentences using all the Vocabulary Words that have three syllables.**

8–10. _____

_____

_____

Harcourt

SCHOOL-HOME CONNECTION Play this game with your child. Say a
sentence in which a Vocabulary Word belongs, but clap instead of saying the
word. Then, guess the word. Take turns playing, using other words in the list.

Name _____

Skill Reminder   **The main idea is the most important point the author is making. Some main ideas are stated in a sentence.**

▶ **Read each paragraph. Then answer the questions.**

It is important to begin the day with a healthy breakfast. Eating right in the morning will help you pay attention in school. It will also give you the energy you need to get through the morning. Finally, eating a healthy breakfast is important for your health.

1. What is the main idea? _____

_____

2. Tell the main idea in your own words. _____

_____

Healthy eating is important for daily life. People of all ages need to eat foods that will give them vitamins and minerals. A good way to know which foods to eat is to follow a food pyramid. Food pyramids help you choose the right food for a healthy meal plan.

3. What is the main idea? _____

_____

4. Tell the main idea in your own words. _____

_____

SCHOOL-HOME CONNECTION With your child, look through some newspapers and find headlines. Discuss what each headline means. Then read the article together to discover if the headline tells the main idea.

Harcourt

Name _____

Skill Reminder **To make an inference, think about what you are reading and what you know from your own experience.**

▶ **Read the passages and the questions. Make inferences to answer each question.**

Fishing for Library Books!

Today was the first day of the "Fishing for Library Books!" contest. Every child who finishes reading a library book gets to put a paper fish on the chart right next to his or her name.

1. Read the title. What do you think this story will be about?

_____

_____

_____

_____

Children can read as many books as they want, and the contest lasts for two months.

2. What do you think a child might have to do to win? _____

_____

At the end of two months, the child with the most fish gets to "fish" for a book.

3. What do you think "fish for a book" means? _____

_____

If you enjoy reading, this is a contest for you.

4. Why should you enjoy reading to enter this contest? _____

_____

 SCHOOL-HOME CONNECTION With your child, think about Ramona, and write words that would help people make some inferences about her character. Discuss your words and Ramona's character.

Harcourt

▶ As you read "Ramona Forever," fill in the boxes below. Remember to fill in the important events in the order in which they happen.

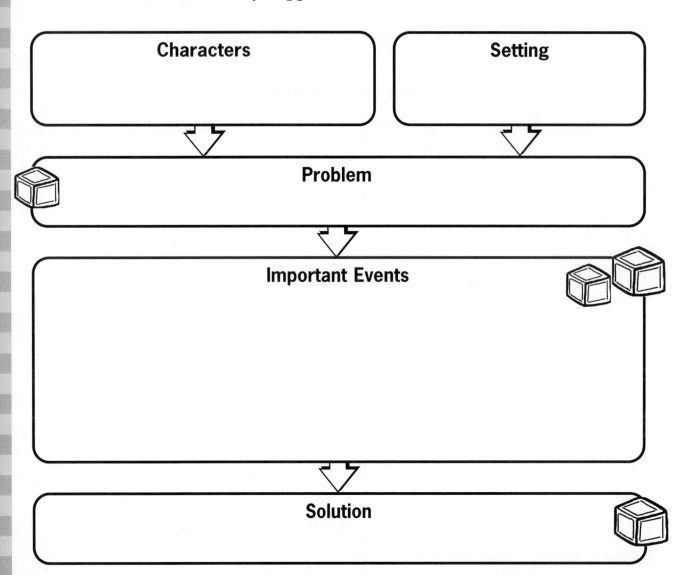

Characters

Setting

Problem

Important Events

Solution

▶ Why does Ramona say that it is hard work to be a baby?

_____

_____

_____

Harcourt

▶ Write *inform, give directions, entertain, persuade,* or *express* to identify the author's purpose for each sentence.

1. Ramona's father does painting for store windows.

_____

2. When you paint, be sure to mix the colors properly and to use even brush strokes.

_____

3. It's great to have a big sister, because she can be a wonderful comfort, especially when she knows how to make you feel safe.

_____

4. Children under twelve are not allowed to visit patients in the hospital.

_____

5. Ramona wiggled like a worm because she began to itch and scratch all over.

_____

6. I think it is hard work to be a baby.

_____

7. Sometimes, babies look cross-eyed until their eyes begin to focus.

_____

8. The hospital should have a special visiting room and waiting room for young children, so they won't feel left out, alone, and scared.

_____

9. Beverly Cleary is the author of "Ramona Forever."

_____

10. Everyone should read books by Beverly Cleary, because she is an imaginative writer who always knows just how to keep the reader interested.

_____

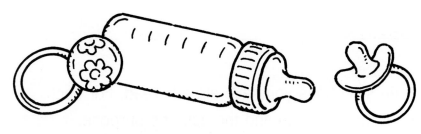

Harcourt

Name _____

► **For each of the following topics, write a sentence for the purpose given.**

Topic	Purpose
1. the library	to persuade

_____

2. washing the dishes   to give directions

_____

3. a television show   to entertain

_____

4. a new baby   to inform

_____

5. an animal   to express

_____

► **List three things you have written, such as a journal entry, and then write your purpose for writing each one.**

6. Writing: _____

     Purpose: _____

7. Writing: _____

     Purpose: _____

8. Writing: _____

     Purpose: _____

TRY THIS! With a partner choose three selections you have already read. For each selection, write the name of the selection and the author's purpose.

Harcourt

Name _____

▶ **Read each sentence. Then choose the correct feeling or action suggested. Write your choice on the line.**

1. The laughing daffodils cheered us up.
happiness or **sorrow**

_____

2. Dark clouds seemed to be having an argument in the sky.
cheerfulness or **anger**

_____

3. The comforting arms of the chair welcomed me.

kindness or **meanness** _____

4. The tree protected the little flowers by giving shade.

selfish or **helpful** _____

5. Like a librarian, the computer guided me to the information I needed.

pride or **helpfulness** _____

6. Holding her head high, the cat left, ignoring us all.

being unfriendly or **being kind** _____

7. The plants cried out for water.

being glad or **being thirsty** _____

8. The old car did not let us down.

being weak or **being trustworthy** _____

 TRY THIS! Write a paragraph about something that makes you happy. Use at least one example of personification in your paragraph.

Name _____

▶ **Write the object pronoun in each sentence.**

1. Tell us more about Ramona. _____

2. The story tells about Beezus and her. _____

3. A new baby sister joined them. _____

4. The girls were brave about it. _____

5. Mr. Quimby's daughters made him proud. _____

▶ **Rewrite each sentence. Use an object pronoun to replace the underlined word or words.**

6. Ramona finally saw <u>Roberta</u>.

_____

7. The baby sucked on <u>one finger</u>.

_____

8. Roberta's face looked red to <u>Ramona and me</u>.

_____

9. Ramona looked at <u>her father</u>.

_____

10. Mr. Quimby smiled at <u>Ramona and Roberta</u>.

_____

 TRY THIS! Write a sentence about you and a friend, using your friend's name and the pronoun *me*. Be sure to use *me* last.

Harcourt

Name _____

▶ **Write the Spelling Words to match the pictures.**

| bear | haircut | airplane | pear |

1. _____

2. _____

3. _____

4. _____

▶ **Write the Spelling Word that best completes each sentence.**

| prepare | stairs | compare | repair |

5. The elevators were crowded, so we used the _____.

6. We need to _____ a list of items to pack.

7. We went to another store to _____ prices.

8. It took three hours to _____ the computer.

Handwriting Tip: Be sure *ar* does not look like *or*.
Write these words.

ar

9. wear _____   **10.** tear _____

SCHOOL-HOME CONNECTION With your child, make up short rhymes using words with the /âr/ sound as in *hair*. Here are some examples: *Please repair the stair. Give the bear a pear. Can you spare a chair?*

Hidden Surprises

Harcourt

Skills and Strategies Index

COMPREHENSION

Draw conclusions 54–55, 60, 70
Homographs and homophones 115
Main idea 106–107, 112, 120
Make inferences 73, 121
Multiple–meaning words 30, 44, 103
Predict outcomes 22–23, 28, 35

Prefixes and suffixes 5–6, 12, 19
Summarizing the literature 4, 13, 21, 29, 37, 45, 53, 62, 72, 80, 87, 94, 105, 114, 122
Synonyms and antonyms 88–89, 95, 104
Vocabulary in context 63–64, 71, 78
Word identification strategies 14, 36

GRAMMAR

Abbreviations 99
Commands and exclamations 25
Common and proper nouns 57
Compound sentences 49
Compound subjects and predicates 41
More plural nouns 75
Object pronouns 126
Plural possessive nouns 91

Sentences 9
Singular and plural nouns 67
Singular and plural pronouns 109
Singular possessive nouns 83
Statements and questions 16
Subject pronouns 117
Subjects and predicates 32

LITERARY APPRECIATION

Author's purpose 123–124
Elements of nonfiction 38–39, 61
Reality and fantasy 81

Story elements–setting, character, and plot 46–47, 52, 79

SPELLING

Consonant blends 42
Possessives and plurals 92
Words with
  /är/ 118
  /âr/ 127
  kn, wr, gh, and *ph* 50
  long *a* and long *e* 26
  long *i* and long *o* 33

/ô/ 100
/oi/ 76
/$\overline{oo}$/ and /o͝o/ 110
/ow/ and /ou/ 84
/s/ and /j/ 68
sh, ch, and *tch* 58
short *a* and short *e* 10
short *i, o,* and *u* 17

STUDY SKILLS

Library/media center 7, 20
Locating information 96–97, 102, 113

Using reference sources 65, 86

VOCABULARY

Abbreviations 48
Classifying 24
Clipped and coined words 98
Compound words 31, 108
Connotation/denotation 56
Jargon and slang 66
Multiple-meaning words 40
Personification 125

Related words 15
Selection vocabulary 3, 11, 18, 27, 34, 43, 51, 59, 69, 77, 85, 93, 101, 111, 119
Signal words 8
Similes 90
Specialized words 82
Vivid verbs 116
Word roots 74